the
INDUSTRIAL
ORDER
and
SOCIAL
POLICY

PRENTICE-HALL SERIES IN SOCIAL POLICY
Howard E. Freeman, Editor

Richard A. Peterson

the
INDUSTRIAL
ORDER
and
SOCIAL
POLICY

prentice-hall, inc.
englewood cliffs, new jersey

For Harold H. Peterson

© 1973 by Prentice-Hall, Inc.
Englewood Cliffs, N. J.

ISBN: P 0-13-464289-9
C 0-13-464297-X

Library of Congress Catalog Card No.: 72-246

10 9 8 7 6 5 4 3 2 1

Printed in the United States of America

PRENTICE-HALL INTERNATIONAL, INC., London
PRENTICE-HALL OF AUSTRALIA, PTY. LTD., Sydney
PRENTICE-HALL OF CANADA, LTD., Toronto
PRENTICE-HALL OF INDIA PRIVATE LIMITED, New Delhi
PRENTICE-HALL OF JAPAN, INC., Tokyo

CONTENTS

87239

PREFACE

We modern peoples rightfully mark our differences from past and peasant peoples by pointing to our great industries, the abundance they provide, and the diverse life styles they make possible. Yet, industrialism, the most obvious product of Western civilization, also provides the means (ranging from nuclear weapons to environmental pollution) which now threaten to destroy our species.

This book is about this industrial revolution but it is neither a scare book nor a program for revolutionary reconstruction. Rather, it is an examination of the industrializing process so that we can begin to shape a more desirable future.

The personal pronoun "we" is often used in the text to convey the feeling that you, the reader, and I together are working through the complex and interesting issues involved. Footnotes—those tributes to archean erudition—have been avoided in order to keep the subject on the track. Authors cited in brackets have dealt with the subject at hand, but all works cited do not necessarily agree with what has been said in the text. Rather, they serve as sources which are relevant to the topic being discussed and may be the basis for further inquiry on the part of the interested reader. Citations in the *Wall Street Journal* are given in order, by date, at the end of the alphabetical bibliography at the back of the book.

RICHARD A. PETERSON
Vanderbilt University

ACKNOWLEDGMENTS

In a sense, this book was started 30 years ago when my father began to spend Sunday mornings talking to me about his experiences. He was then an executive in Johns-Manville Corporation and many of his stories had to do with the variety of people and processes that make up an international industrial firm. At one time or another over a 10 year period he talked on a wide range of subjects. These included the founding of the firm, production techniques, product development, negotiation with labor unions, the newspaper coverage of industrial accidents, rivalries between sales divisions, the indelicacies of women workers, dismantling a company-owned town, financing new office buildings, the game of executive advancement and demotion, conflict with French Catholic priests, many of the reasons why men work, and the causes of industrial accidents. Taken together, the conversations gave the impression of a corporation as a social enterprise which is a potent force in the lives of individuals, entire communities, and the society at large. Many of his insights, gained from years of experience, have been codified and appear in the work which follows in more general sociological terms.

A number of teachers and colleagues have given my interest in industry a more sociological focus and sharpened my tool of inquiry over the last 20 years. Those who have been most influential along the way include: Maurice Stein who, at Oberlin College, demonstrated that sociology could be both useful and fun; Alvin W. Gouldner who, at the University of Illinois and over the years since, has shown me something of what the critical-intellectual-research enterprise should be; the University of Wisconsin "Junior Jury" (including most noteably Bob Alford, Milt Bloombaum, Jay Demerath, Joe Elder, Kreel Fromann, Warren Hagstrom, Jack Ladinsky, Stan Lieberson, Gerry Marwell, David Mechanic, Nelson Polsby, Tom Scheff, and Allan Silver) which rendered into usable form many an over-fat research idea; Harry V. Ball and the Russell-Sage Foundation who gave me intellectual, emotional, and financial support while I was formulating this project. I also wish to acknowledge my colleagues at Vanderbilt University during these vintage years of the department—especially Mayer N. Zald who has been the model of colleagueship; and, those students who have been engaged in one or another aspect of the enterprise. Their work is cited where it is relevant in the text.

I would especially like to think Robert Boguslaw, James D. Thompson, Claire L. Peterson, Mayer N. Zald, and that most patient of editors, Howard E. Freeman, who have carefully read the manuscript. In addition I would like to thank Howard Becker, R. Serge Denisoff, John McCarthy, Harold Wilensky, and Charles P. Wolf who have been most helpful with one or another part of this work.

the
INDUSTRIAL
ORDER
and
SOCIAL
POLICY

Chapter 1

THE CRUCIBLE OF INDUSTRY

Modern man is uniquely Industrial Man. Modern society has been manufactured, and its institutions continue to be transformed by the processes of industrialization. This book focuses on the social consequences of the continuing industrial revolution so that we can bring the process more completely under human control.

The Image

Many symbols of industrialization have captured the popular imagination. But perhaps none has been so powerful an image of the total process as the huge, hot, dangerous steel mill. Here various types of rock are thrown into the crucible and, under conditions of barely controlled violence, rendered into a uniform product which takes on a multitude of forms under the eyes of machine-equipped men working in close coordination. The boats, trains, shovels, furnaces, and other machines used in this transformation are of colossal proportions as are the corporate organizations required to coordinate them.

It has proved impossible to segregate the crucible of industry from other aspects of human existence. In practice, none of the attempts to gain fruits of modernization without industrialization, such as Gandhi's plan to destroy the Indian caste system, or efforts to gain industrialization without introducing its social correlates as was tried by the nineteenth century leaders of Japan, has long been successful (Bendix 1956; Smelser 1959; W. Moore 1965; B. Moore 1966; Eisenstadt 1966; Lenski 1966). As we will show in the chapters which follow, changes in the industrial order are predicated on and in turn cause changes in politics, religion, the family, art, values, and even the very conception of what it means to be human.

DON QUIXOTE RIDES AGAIN

One of the leading ideas in the transformation process has been that man and society are not fated to a particular order, that by planning destiny can be changed. Such planning is now widely practiced but much of it has a quality akin to the designs of that great fictional character, Don Quixote.

That impoverished late medieval Spanish gentleman-farmer and avid reader of novels about knightly chivalry tried to transform his own desultory world into that ideal about which he had read. In one of his early adventures he charged headlong into a windmill, imagining it to be an evil giant who was blocking his way. His body bruised, his horse fallen, and his lance shattered, he explained to his perplexed companion, Sancho Panza, that a malevolent sorcerer had temporarily transformed the giant into a windmill in order to rob him of the glory of vanquishing the giant. While this is the story of a crazed man it is also, at another level, a story of revolutionary combat, for the wind-powered gristmill was equivalent to the computer today. It was the most conspicuous early practical machine designed to harness the forces of nature for industrial production. The knightly Don Quixote represented the failing power of the landed aristocracy which would be supplanted by industrialization. Thus, the good knight correctly identified his adversary, but being completely steeped in the mystique of chivalry and magic he was impotent in combating it or shaping it to his ends. What is more, his belief in magic made it possible to rationalize his failure without ever understanding it.

We, alas, are in very little better position today for we are often blinded to the changing realities around us by outmoded ways of thinking about the problems which lie across *our* path. For this reason, this brief book is as concerned with examining the various ideas about how to guide the industrialization process as it is with describing the industrial order.

EARLY PERSPECTIVES ON SOCIAL PLANNING

The attempt to understand society and plan social change is an age-old quest; what is new is the framework within which questions are being asked. Medieval and early modern scholars, more or less freeing themselves of the idea that the social order was directly manipulated by God, identified the political domain as the natural frame of reference for their study. Their prime question concerned the proper relationship of individuals and organizations to government. This "political" orientation is equally characteristic of scholars as diverse in their cultural and religious convictions as Thomas Aquinas (1225–1274), Iban Khaldun (1332–1406), Niccolo Machiavelli (1469–1527), Jean Bodin (1530–1596), Thomas Hobbes (1588–1679), Charles Montesquieu (1689–1775), David Hume (1711–1776), and Jean Jacques Rousseau (1712–1778). These theorists were concerned with *economic* matters, only insofar as they related to political questions.

The theory called *mercantilism* exemplifies this tendency of seeing economic questions in terms of the state apparatus. Economic stability was necessary, the mercantilists argued, to guarantee state revenues and to maintain domestic tranquility. The limit of economic development was bounded by a hand tool technology, organized in terms of an anti-innovative craft system of work roles and buttressed by the communalistic values of medieval Catholicism. Thus, the productive capacity of a territory was assumed to be relatively fixed. The first major break with this intellectual focus on political questions and a static economy came with the rising importance of commercial capitalism, which developed first in Italy and spread around the Atlantic edge of Europe. Gradually a new theory emerged which argued for commerce and industry "unfettered" by governmental and traditional restraints. This view, now called *classical economics,* was given its first full expression in Adam Smith's *Wealth of Nations,* published in 1776.

Classical Economics. Adam Smith argued that the wealth of any nation depends not on fixed properties such as land and gold, but on the productive capacity of its citizens. This capacity is, in turn, dependent upon the degree of specialization of the labor force; for the greater the division of labor, the more productive each worker is, since he can then perfect a single skill rather than having to be competent in several. As Smith noted, "In consequence of the division of labor, the whole of every man's attention comes naturally to be directed toward some very simple object. It is naturally to be expected, therefore, that someone or other of those who are employed in each branch of labor should soon find easier and readier methods of performing their own particular work" (1776:9).* Thus, the division of labor is a spur to invention.

Smith goes on to observe that the division of labor depends on the size of the market; the wider the market, the greater the division of labor and use of specialized tools and, consequently, the lower the cost of production per unit produced. Smith drew his prime example to illustrate these "economics of scale" from the newly introduced mass production of straight pins.

---

*Numbers within parentheses refer to year and page number in the work cited. References are listed alphabetically by the author's name at the end of this book. Unauthored articles in the *Wall Street Journal* are listed by date at the end of the alphabetical listing.

Since the wealth of any nation depends on its productive capacity according to this theory, any government restriction on the working of the free market, through tariffs or the protection of monopolies, reduces the aggregate rational wealth by supporting less efficient producers. The mechanism which should control the level of production is the unseen hand of the perfectly competitive market. According to this theory the economic function of the government is to prevent the creation of private monopolies which are in restraint of free trade; these were, even in 1776, a persistent danger. As Smith observed, those active "in the same trade seldom meet together but the conversation ends in a conspiracy against the public" (1776:289). Beyond this, he argued, government should provide the legal and monetary framework within which orderly economic activity can take place, thus encouraging business activity *in general* without favoring any segment *in particular.*

Smith was not insensitive to the disruptive consequences of the division of labor. For example, in one telling passage he notes: "The understandings of the greater part of men are necessarily formed by their ordinary employment. The man whose whole life is spent in performing a few simple operations...has no occasion to exert his understandings.... He naturally loses therefore the habit of such exertion, and generally becomes as stupid and ignorant as it is possible for a human creature to become...his dexterity at his own particular trade seems, in this manner, to be acquired at the expense of his intellecutal, social, and marital virtues. But in very improved and civilized society this is the state into which the laboring poor, that is, the great body of the people must necessarily fall, *unless government takes some pains to prevent it"* (1776:734). While Smith did suggest that the government provide education to counteract the stultifying influences of the workplace, he did not elaborate this idea or trace the further ramifications of the division of labor outside the workplace.

SOCIOLOGY—CHILD OF THE INDUSTRIAL REVOLUTION

The next generation of scholars could hardly escape this task, as a number of riots, risings, and disorders—most notably the French Revolution—brought to popular attention the multifaceted consequences of the Industrial Revolution which was fundamentally transforming Western society. While craftsmen often resorted to direct action, breaking the machines which made irrelevant their craft skills, traditionally oriented scholars decried the new mechanization. They saw in the growing wealth of industrialists a weakening of the power of the landed aristocracy and town merchants, as well as the enfeeblement of the medieval craft guilds. The political economists shared Adam Smith's pessimistic view of the dehumanizing consequences of factory work.

At the same time, a growing number of scholars began to study the Industrial Revolution as a social process, with hopes of being able to speed its development while mitigating its negative consequences. Their optimism was based on the idea that by using *reason* and applying the methods of science to social affairs man could come to understand and thus control societal change. This is the basic ambiance of the sociological tradition. While Auguste Comte (1798–1857), Karl Marx (1818–1884), and Herbert Spencer (1820–1903) hardly agreed on what particular social policy should be followed, they saw the Industrial Revolution as a great advance in society, worthy of close study so that the proper social policies regarding it could be followed.

Saint-Simon. The ideas that comprise the sociological tradition can be found in the works of many men, but many received their first systematic expression in the works of Henri Compte de Saint-Simon (1760–1825). His family had been influential advisors in the French courts of Louis XIII and XIV. As a youth he served with the French expeditionary forces in the American Revolution and later, during the French Revolutoin, shed his noble title and made a fortune speculating in confiscated church properties. He then devoted himself to the problems of industrialization and social reform, becoming the center of an informal group of utopian planners. His works include *The Industrial System* and *A Political Catechism for Industrialists.*

Like Adam Smith, Saint-Simon saw the division of labor as the primary social aspect of the Industrial Revolution. But he went beyond Smith in tracing its consequences for political and social institutions including the government, social stratification, religion and the family. He saw social planning as one of the prime *imperatives* of industrialization, and had great faith in the development of rational human action in implementing planned social change. Thus, Saint-Simon brought together many of the key ideas that would constitute the sociological domain for scholars like Comte, Marx, Spencer, Durkheim, Simmel, Weber, Sumner, Ward, and Veblen (Durkheim 1958; Manuel 1956; Hansen 1966). These men, and the academic discipline they built, continue to focus on the scientific *study* of industrial society in order to work for its continual *perfection.*

Karl Marx characterized Saint-Simon as "utopian" because of his focus on a distant glorious future. Saint-Simon believed that the reconstruction of society would come through the interjection of one major new factor into society (industrialization), that change would occur more or less automatically and, insofar as active planning was necessary, it would be done for the good of all by an emerging industrial-intellectual elite (Zeitlin 1968:59).

Contemporary Utopians. A number of contemporary planners can be called "utopian" in just this same sense. Modern utopians most often look for a change in technology or in values. Some see technology producing a horn of plenty (Kahn and Wiener 1967) and creating a benign computer-based knowledge (Boguslaw 1965), while others see an emerging consciousness which will make inconsequential traditional forms of conflict (Reich 1970; Nobile 1971). Marshall McLuhan (1962) combines these perspectives in asserting that key changes in technology are creating a new consciousness.

In an indictment parallel to that made by Marx against Saint-Simon, Ferkiss (1970:22–28) faults these *new* utopians for their single factor theories of change, the mechanistic determinism involved in change, and their preoccupation with the future desired state of affairs. The utopian futurists' stance allows these men to cast aside as transitory and epiphenomenal such problems as civil war, unemployment, drug addiction, third world upheaval, and environmental pollution. Convenient as it would be, there is no evidence in the lessons of the past or the present to suggest that these vexing problems will dissolve. In fact, it is likely that the new technological marvels will cause the incineration of the human species in a nuclear holocaust or lead to its suffocation through pollution.

Toward a Self-Controlling Society

Moving from the present toward a *desirable* future, Etzioni (1968:1–16) argues, will not just happen. It will necessitate our taking an *active* part in creating knowledge of social processes and planning for change. In agreeing with Etzioni, we must clarify two issues, the meaning of the term "planning" and the question of who will plan and towards what ends.

To Plan: A Transitive Verb. The prospect of a planned economy or planned society raises the image of a totalitarian plan promulgated by a central government agency for the entire nation. As has been pointed out by Galbraith (1967), such centralized planning is as quixotic as would be a real venture in *non*planning in the laissez faire tradition because of the complexities of contemporary technologies, high levels of education, political sophistication, and wealth of modern American society. We will, rather, advocate the sort of planning which has begun to emerge in this past decade. It involves planning by a wide range of autonomous units ranging in size from corporations to individual families who compete for relative advantage within the framework of American legal and political institutions. In this design the government does not plan so much as it helps to maintain an environment in which others can successfully plan. Thus we will argue for government policies that will make possible the kind of planning in our postindustrial society that is consonant with the fundamental American values placed on equality and freedom.

The "Social Problem" Problem. In the industrial sphere questions of who plans and for what ends are not easily solved for two related reasons.

First, there is no agreement on what the problems are, and second, any change has a number of consequences which may be harmful to some interests while helpful to others. This dilemma can be seen as the "Social Problem" problem.

That certain behavior or a state of affairs is a social problem is not inherent in the phenomenon itself. The designation "social problem" involves a value judgment (Merton and Nisbet 1971; Horowitz 1968:80–100; Kavolis 1969:1–6). Several social scientists have suggested that a social problem *is* what people define as a problem. For example, Robert Dentler states, "A social problem is a condition that has been defined by significant groups as a deviation from social standards, or breakdown of social organization" (1967:15). If everyone agrees that a problem exists there is little practical difficulty with this definition. That heroin addiction, for example, is a problem which should be solved is agreed upon by doctors, public authorities, society at large, and even the addict himself. Only those involved in the intricate and highly profitable industry which supplies narcotics would disagree with the "social problem" value judgment. Since this industry is illegal and is usually defined as contributing nothing to society, social scientists find little difficulty in treating drug addiction as a social problem (O'Donnell and Ball 1966; Cressey 1969).

The case is quite different when it comes to the process of industrialization. It would be easy to show that it causes far more injury and privation than drug addiction and all other sorts of personal crimes combined. There are, for example, established relationships between certain sorts of jobs and specific mental ills. (Kornhauser 1964; Simmons 1965; Baker, McEwen, and Sheldon 1969). At the same time, technological change often makes obsolete those skills which have been gained over a lifetime, just as factory relocation may destroy a business or a whole town (Cottrell 1951; Aiken 1968; Anderson 1968). While industrialization may be destructive to health, status, and property, it is difficult to use the social problem frame of reference, for the activity which may be a problem to one individual or group is likely to mean profit for another. Let us focus briefly on one example which illustrates this fact.

PROBLEMS AND PROFIT IN BEEF: AN ILLUSTRATION

Today the vast livestock market of Chicago is nearly a ghost town. The huge multistory meat packing plants described by Blum (1953) either have shut down or are operating at a loss, and the great firms of the industry, Swift and Armour, have lost much business. Thousands of workers have lost their jobs in the plants, and many auxiliary concerns have gone out of business. At the same time, many meat companies which did not exist ten years ago have moved into positions of prominence in the beef industry. One of these, a company called Iowa Beef Packers is now the largest processor of grain-fed beef in the country.

The success of these new companies which has been described in "Everything but the Moo" (Pacey 1968), depends upon a number of inter-related innovations in technology, organization, and marketing. The new slaughterhouses are located in small towns spread over the countryside in cattle fattening areas. Since it is more convenient for local farmers to sell to only one slaughterhouse rather than to ship to the larger open markets, the slaughtering companies can more easily dictate beef prices.

A number of these new plants have been built with special tax-free industrial development bonds floated to attract the industry to towns such as Dakota City, Nebraska. In effect, the federal government has subsidized the geographical dispersion of packing plants through these tax breaks while, at the same time, workers in Chicago and Kansas City draw unemployment insurance payments and press for government-sponsored job retraining (Kovack 1965; Janssen 1968). Packing companies find another advantage in moving to smaller towns; the work population tends to be more stable, rates of pay lowers, and unions less militant, so that there is less resistance to mechanize operations further.

Innovations in Production. These new slaughterhouses have incorpo-rated a number of innovations in production as well. In the past, most of the nation's beef was slaughtered and quartered, and then shipped to retail butcher shops. In an Iowa Beef Packers plant slaughtering proceeds as usual until the workers, stationed on each side of a long conveyor-topped table, divide the freshly slaughtered carcasses into seven basic cuts. These cuts are graded and packaged in plastic film, then moved along a complex of con-veyors to refrigerated areas where they are reassembled and boxed as whole beefs. Since there is some degree of latitude in how beef is cut, a company computer has been programmed to take into account the fluctuating rela-tive prices of different cuts to determine exactly how carcasses should be sectioned for maximum profit.

With each increase in factory fabrication and prepackaging of meat there is less need for skilled butchers in the thousands of retail outlets around the country. Since butchers have become technologically unemployed, their union has strongly resisted factory fabrication. On the other hand, store owners favor prepackaging because two-thirds of a retail grocery store's equipment expenses are in the meat department, and the elimination of retail meat processing would sharply reduce store overhead.

Not only does the vacuum packaging in plastic greatly reduce the activity of bacteria, thus increasing the shelf-life of cut meat from twelve to twenty-one days, but the technology which makes plastic packaging possible is easily adapted to quick freezing the meat. Frozen meat can be kept six months, and since the aging process continues through this period, it tastes better after six months than when it was frozen. The prime barrier to introducing this frozen meat processing is not technology or organization of the corporation, but rather the antipathy of housewives in buying frozen beef. Seeing this as a social problem, ten years ago the Swift Company tried "educating" housewives to buy frozen meat but suffered heavy losses on the venture. Other companies are reluctant to repeat this experiment, for if they are successful in selling frozen meat, other companies can quickly change over and reap the benefits at no risk. From the point of view of the treasurer of Iowa Beef Producers, "It's archaic for a woman to expect meat to be cut especially for her in a modern supermarket. She buys frozen turkey because she has no choice, and the beef people shouldn't give her a choice either" (Pacey 1968:8).

The Sight and Smell of Profit. Although citizens of the new packing towns complain about the pungent odor noticeable within miles of any meat processing plant, they are told by Iowa officials that this is the smell of jobs and money for the town. As an executive explained, "When there's no smell the town isn't making money" (Pacey 1968:3). Iowa Beef Packers accents its focus on money by painting the offices, trucks, and packing houses green, inside and out; desks, typewriters, and carpeting follow the monochromatic scheme.

Do the current changes taking place in the beef industry constitute a social problem? If we follow Dentler's assertion that a social problem is what people define as a problem, then the Chicago packing house workers and butchers around the country who have lost their source of livelihood, as well as those people who live within olfactory range of the new plants, see this as a social problem. It is clearly not a problem for those who profit from the success of the new companies like Iowa Beef Packers. As this example suggests, the social problem frame of reference is just not very helpful for examining the processes of industrialization unless it is broadened from the level of individual and group interests to the level of social functioning. The perspective taken in this book will be to view the continuing process of industrialization *itself* as a social problem.

Outline of the Book

Initially we will draw many illustrations from the early phases of the Industrial Revolution in the belief that many of our current problems parallel those of the past and can best be understood by being viewed in a comparative perspective. With this in mind, Chapter 2 introduces a number of concepts and shows the relationships among them by tracing the early phases of the Industrial Revolution in the "Satanic" textile mills of England. Chapter 3 brings the historical line forward to the present by tracing some of the problems which arise from the contemporary technologies of mass production and automation.

While Chapters 2 and 3 are set in historical perspective, the succeeding chapters are more topical. Chapter 4 focuses on contemporary forms of industrial organizations in the industrial sphere. These range from massive conglomerate corporations to self-employed taxicab drivers, from decadent labor unions to the current organizational activities of agricultural workers in California. Chapter 5 focuses on contemporary work from the perspective of an individual caught in the crucible of industry. The concept of alienation is introduced, its origins are sought, and the many techniques directed at its amelioration are outlined.

While the first five chapters are devoted to description and analysis, Chapter 6 is a consideration of means proposed to solve some of the problems introduced by the process of industrialization. Rather than offer a particular solution, Chapter 6 points to an intellectual perspective which can be useful in bringing the process of industrialization more fully under human control.

Chapter 2

THE INDUSTRIAL REVOLUTION

This chapter has two general aims. The first is to define some of the concepts which are used throughout the rest of the book. These include technology, social structure, and ideology. The second aim is to show some of the interconnections between these. Illustrations are drawn from the early phases of the Industrial Revolution, which gathered sustained momentum in England after 1750, because it is often possible to see a general process more clearly when one is not caught up in them as current events. This history is of more than antiquarian interest, however, because many of the dilemmas faced in the early phases of the Industrial Revolution have their parallels today.

Orientation

While there are innumerable ways of looking at something as complex as the Industrial Revolution, all approaches deal, in one way or another with technology, social structure, and values. It is imperative to understand these elements and suggest their interrelationships.

TECHNOLOGY DEFINED

Following the general usage proposed by Karl Mannheim (1941:243–52), technology is defined as the relationship between materials, tools or machines, and skills or procedures. Seen in this perspective, there is as surely a technology of making a president of the United States as there is of making an Oldsmobile or a jet aircraft. Since we are interested in the crucible of industry, this book focuses on those technologies which involve the manufacture and distribution of goods or services for sale—that is, industrial technology.

Inherent in this definition is the distinction between *machine* technology involving the processing of tools and machines, on the one hand, and *social* technology involving the skills and means of organizing people to get work done on the other. This dichotomy parallels the distinction made by Karl Marx between the machine *forces* of production and the social *relations* of production. The distinction between machine and social technology can be seen in an example; in medieval Europe the machine technology included simple farming and craft tools powered by man and beast, augmented by simple mechanical leverage. The social techniques of the era included the Manorial system of agricultural production and the guild system of organizing the production and distribution of goods.

One of the defining elements of the Industrial Revolution was the substitution of inanimate for animate sources of power. This involved the harnessing of wind and water and, later, steam, electric, and atomic energy. These changes in machine technology were accompanied by dramatic changes in social technology. Most scholars presume that changes in material technology precede changes in social technology (Ogburn 1933, 1946; Landes 1969), but this is by no means always the case.

For example, the introduction of factory production which made possible the development of power-driven machinery, was the product of changes in social technology. In the early part of the eighteenth century, English textile goods were manufactured on hand looms in the home (Mantoux 1961; Henderson 1969). Traveling entrepreneurs called "factors" brought the raw cotton to the homes of workers scattered over the countryside and carried off the finished yard goods. Family members were in charge of all aspects of production under the direction of the family head. This form of "cottage industry," called in England the "putting-out" system, was quite inefficient. For example, the factor had no great control over the quality or the quantity of goods produced. Family members worked when they were free from agricultural pursuits and when they needed cash income, and not in accord with the nuances of market demand.

In order to gain more control in the process of production, factors began to gather numbers of workers together under their control in a place which came to be called a "factory." With full-time wage workers employed in a factory, it became practical to tinker with the tools of textile manufacturing. In the process of innovation, machines quickly became heavier, faster, and more efficient, taxing the power of men to operate them by hand. Very soon power was drawn from falling water, and experimental steam engines were developed. Thus the radical restructuring of the social technology of textile production—locating workers in factories—was a direct *stimulant* which made economically feasible systematic tinkering with the machine technology.

SOCIAL STRUCTURE

Having introduced two kinds of technology, let us briefly explore the meaning of the concept, "social structure." In this context, it will include institutions such as family, education, leisure, religion, and government; as well as social processes such as stratification, communication, socialization, and social control, together constituting the domain which sociologists characterize as *social*.

The term *structure* implies that these elements are interrelated in *patterns*. Three ideas follow from this notion of pattern. First, a given type of institution is compatible only with a narrow range of alternatives in other institutional areas. It has been argued that the Industrial Revolution began in England in part because of the presence of particular political and religious institutions (Bendix 1956).

Second, alternative elements may fulfill the function of original elements, so that there is not an exact and predetermined fit between elements of the social structure. Thus, for example, there are different ways of accumulating the wealth necessary to finance industrial development—a process called capital formation. The eighteenth century Protestant value placed on individual savings, frugality, and hard work operated in England as the means of capital formation necessary for industrial development. In Russia both under the Tsars and Soviets, on the other hand, capital formation has been more completely in the hands of the central state. Through taxes, expropriation, wage and price controls, the state has tried to manage the aggregation and investment of capital. As means of accumulating large amounts of capital for industrial development, the English and Russian systems are what Robert K. Merton (1968:67–90) has called "functional alternatives." These two alternatives, of course, have quite different impacts on other aspects of their respective societies such as politics and religion.

Finally, the idea of pattern suggests that the change of any one element in the system will have consequences for other elements. As we saw in the example of the meat packing industry, some of the ramifying changes are intended while others are not. What is more, some consequences are anticipated by those in the situation while many are not.

Immigration Policy: An Example. The changing United States policy toward immigration provides several good illustrations of both unintended and unanticipated consequences (Blaug 1969:241–301). Throughout most of the nation's early history persons were allowed to immigrate freely to this country. This policy was intended both to afford a haven in the new world from poverty and oppression and to provide a steady stream of new recruits to American factories. By the close of the last century and the first decade of this, however, free immigration was having the unanticipated and unintended effect of changing the ethnic and religious composition of the population: northern European Protestant immigrants were largely replaced by southern and eastern European Catholics and Jews. At the close of World War I an immigration law was enacted which set strict national quotas. Its intention was to have a mix of immigrants corresponding roughly with the composition of the United States population of 1870. Thus, for example, the annual quota for England was quite large while that for Poland was quite small.

In the 1960s this legislation was attacked as "racially motivated"— which it was. In 1966 a new immigration law was enacted which enlarged the immigration quotas from the nations of Asia, Africa, Latin America, and the underdeveloped world generally. A provision of the new act gave preference to potential immigrants with scarce and critical skills. This was intended to aid the national security of the United States. The consequence has been an increased "brain drain" of the most intelligent and best trained scientists, doctors, technicians, and engineers from the underdeveloped world. The inflow of physicians and scientists has been substantial. According to a government report (*Washington Newsletter* 1968:8) the number of physicians entering the United States in 1967 equaled the total year's output of the country's fifteen largest medical schools. Yet the gain to the United States in this exchange is slight in comparison to the incalculable loss of the underdeveloped countries. According to the report it cost the developing world at least $150 million to educate the 7,913 scientists, engineers, and physicians who immigrated to the United States in 1967. The report warned that if the United States (and other advanced countries) continued to encourage this brain drain, the developing world would suffer long-term consequences from the erosion of a relatively small cadre of trained leadership personnel, a consequence which was unintended and probably unanticipated by the framers of United States immigration policy.

This view of social structure as a system has been criticized by many authors over the years (cf. Demerath and Peterson 1967), but it remains a useful device for organizing ideas about the impact of a continuing industrial revolution on all aspects of society. Such a global approach is taken by some writers of industrial sociology textbooks, most notably (Form and Miller 1960; Shostak 1969; and Schneider 1969). The still unexcelled study of the links between industry and the rest of community life are Robert and Helen Lynd's two studies of Muncie, Indiana (1929, 1937). While we will show some of the links between industry and family, education, religion, leisure, stratification, race, the mass media, war, and the like, the prime focus will be on industry's many interconnections with the political institution because we are, in this book, ultimately concerned with the policies by which we may bring the process of industrialization more nearly under human control.

VALUES AND IDEOLOGY

Whenever one makes a choice, he is expressing a value. The arts, material well-being, religious speculation, military exploits, and productive work are valued in most industrialized societies. Different societies, however, place greater *relative* worth on one or another of these values.

Individuals in all societies learn to strive for their own advantage, and for the family and the wider groups to which they belong. Yet the values of all societies place constraints on these acquisitive quests, inhibiting technological innovation. For example, in Dobuan society, located on a barren island with a subsistence economy, the large harvest of an individual is taken as *prima facie* evidence that he has magically stolen the crops from his closest neighbors. Thus, what we would call a *good* (meaning large) harvest, they see as an *illegal* harvest stolen from other people (Benedict 1934). In such a society there is little incentive to work in an effort to increase crop yields.

Many societies believe that great wealth can only be gained by crime and cunning at the expense of others who must suffer as a consequence. In medieval European society this idea was the basis for the moral condemnation of almost all forms of commercial profit as "usury" (Meislin and Cohen 1964; Lane 1964). In most societies there is little incentive for men to acquire capital. Needy relatives and neighbors demand the right to share the wealth. Given such values, there is little profit in innovation, hard work, and saving; rather, it is much more rational for a man to be generous with his bounty in the anticipation that others will reciprocate when he is in need (Banfield 1958; Erasmus 1961; Belshaw 1965; Dalton 1967; Nash 1966).

Ideology. By way of illustrating the transformation from religion-dominated values to property-dominated values which accompanied the Industrial Revolution, Marx notes that just when the English gave up the practice of burning witches, they began to hang the forgers of bank notes. Nineteenth century American society gave particularly high place to innovative, unscrupulous, hard working, self-made men (Diamond 1966). Yet these men of new wealth, such as Jim Fisk, John D. Rockefeller and Russell Sage, would be considered little better than scum to a medieval Catholic or to a citizen of most ancient civilizations of the world (Tawney 1937; Weber 1958).

Values are best measured in the choices people make among alternatives. At the same time people often go to great lengths to justify, explain, and rationalize the choices they make. Such rationalizations we will call *ideology*. Ideology and values may coincide, but they often differ in interesting ways. A striking illustration is provided by the fact that for at least two centuries American businessmen have verbalized an ideology of private free enterprise based on competition, unrestricted by government control; however, most of their business activities reflect a higher *value* placed on having monopolistic control of the market, and they often seek the protection of local, state, and national governments to limit competition (Sutton, Harris, Kaysen, and Tobin 1956; Diamond 1966; Bunting 1964). A most dramatic instance of this Janus-faced posture of ideology versus value among businessmen is the continual pronouncements concerning the value of competition, together with strenuous efforts to build and defend high tariff barriers against free competition (Bauer, Pool, and Dexter 1963).

Ideological statements may be fabricated for the moment's convenience but, quite often, over the course of time, they become sincerely believed and thus become a basis for action. As Bendix (1959: 619) has noted, "Ideology often fixes a vocabulary and the grammar for the ways people think." A most striking illustration of this process can be drawn from United States history. The Declaration of Independence from English rule was framed in order to gain as much popular support as possible for the cause of the secessionists. The assertion that "all men are created equal" probably was not intended to include women, and certainly was not intended to include blacks. Yet the memorizing of this line by generations of citizens has fixed the more general notion as a legitimate right, and it is now difficult to argue against granting it to blacks and women who increasingly claim equality as their right as Americans.

Ideology may shape behavior in yet other ways. For example, actions taken in accordance with the dictates of one ideological position may have unintended consequences. For a striking instance of this we return to our earlier example of the textile industry in England. The predominately conservative English Parliament, between 1700 and 1748, passed a number of laws with the announced intention of preserving the preindustrial system of production based on craft guild labor. These laws had the effect, however, of greatly speeding the process of industrialization (Mantoux 1961; Bendix 1956). In later sections we will examine in detail several such examples of conservatives advancing the process of the Industrial Revolution while intending to retard it.

Tension Creates Ideology. A number of authors have observed that ideology does not develop in all areas of human activity to the same degree. Rather, ideology is elaborated around points of tension and change (Sutton, Harris, Kaysen, and Tobin 1956). Thus the study of ideology is not only interesting in itself but also serves much as fever serves a doctor; as an index of pathology to signal a tension point or element of society undergoing rapid change. For example, Huizinga (1954), in his excellent book on the intellectual and artistic mode of the late Middle Ages, notes a rising concern on the part of royal court moralists with the newly important sins of pride and cupidity. Pride involved the assumption of noble prerogatives by those less worthy, and cupidity involved an unseemly lusting after wealth. From the point of view of the *landed* gentry, both were sins of the rising *commercial* middle class. An analysis of this ideology would sensitize one to the struggle of the newly wealthy commercial class against the established landed interests. We will study the elaboration of ideology as a symptom of deeper tensions in several later chapters.

TECHNOLOGICAL DETERMINISM?

Having defined several of the key concepts which we will be using, we might ask about their interrelations. To begin with, is a given material technology associated with a particular form of social technology? The answer, from available sources, would seem to be positive (Heilbroner 1962). Wherever we find assembly line production, in Russia, Japan, South America, or the United States for example, we also find a social technology based on quite similar bureaucratic principles. What is more, this same rigid set of bureaucratic arrangements is altered wherever automation is introduced.

The link between technology and elements of the social structure, such as government, family, and education, is not so direct, but it appears that only a limited *range* of alternatives are possible for any given technology (Bendix 1956; Smelser 1963; Moore 1963, 1965; Eisenstadt 1966; Udy 1970). We will return to this point in several contexts later in the book. When we turn to the link between technology and ideology the evidence is much less clear. A number of researchers have been fascinated with this question, particularly as it concerns the conflict between capitalism and communism (Heilbroner 1967). Put most briefly, the question may be phrased: do the constraints of technology make industrial nations increasingly alike by eliminating, or at least rendering irrelevant, the ideological antagonisms between capitalism and communism?

Scholars are divided on the question. Philosophically oriented historians and most economists see a real convergence of technology and a withering away of ideological differences (Rostow 1962; Galbraith 1967; Meier 1966). Technical historians and anthropologists tend to see a continuing cultural-ideological diversity in spite of technological convergence (Spicer 1952; Nash 1966). Those sociologists who focus on the industrial processes tend to see real convergence (Inkeles 1960; Feldman and Moore 1961; Moore 1965); while those who focus on social and political phenomena tend to see a continuing diversity (Moore 1966; Bendix 1956; Eisenstadt 1966;

Crozier 1964). Whatever the resolution of this great issue few follow Clark Kerr, Dunlop, Harbison, and Myers (1961) in predicting that technical, social, and ideological convergences between nations will soon make for a harmonizing of internation differences and the elimination of the threat of war.

Growth is not Inevitable. Many authors have been fascinated with a kind of technological determinism, most often called the "technological imperative." In their view early technological advances have many ramifying consequences for social structure, values, and ideology. These changes, they argue, make continuing advances in technology inevitable so that economic and social growth become built-in mechanisms of industrial societies. Within this context Walter Rostow (1962) has talked of five stages of economic growth which evolve naturally once industrialization has begun. Using data from the United States, northern Europe, and Japan, an impressive case can be constructed, but there are a number of nations which do not fit the progression (Eisenstadt 1964).

Perhaps the outstanding case which goes against the thesis of technological imperative is Argentina (Stavenhagen 1967; Fillol 1967; Bradby 1969). In most ways its potential for rapid industrialization after 1880 was far superior to that of a number of nations including Japan. It had a broad, fertile territory, rich natural resources, rapid immigration of skilled workers, stable government, and a thriving agricultural industry with sufficient exports to finance industrialization. Industry grew rapidly in the final decades of the nineteenth century. Yet, the progress of industrialization since has been sporatic and, in the decades since World War II, almost nil. For example between 1950 and 1958, when most other advanced nations experienced annual growth rates between three and seven percent, Argentina had a cumulative growth rate of only 1.7 percent. In half the years since 1958 the growth rate has actually been negative! A complete explanation of this stagnation has not been given, but the Argentine case does put the lie to any facile assertion of a "technological imperative."

CHANGING TECHNOLOGY AS REVOLUTION

As Faunce (1965, 1968) has noted, the aspects of physical or machine technology can be subdivided into several elements. These include applying inanimate sources of power to the production process, developing the machinery of materials handling, and mechanizing quality control and decision making. While developments in these areas may occur independently, Faunce asserts a certain level of development of each is necessary for the further development of the others. In general, the first stages of the Industrial Revolution involve the application of power to the production processes and the perfection of sophisticated specialized *machines* of production, as exemplified in the early textile industry. The second stage focuses on the mechanization of *materials handling* techniques as exemplified in the automobile assembly line. The third stage focuses on the technology of production *control,* as exemplified by the computer and other related paraphernalia of automation.

The remaining section of this chapter and all of the next will deal with these three stages in turn, but one final remark needs to be made on the meaning of the term "revolution" as it is used in relation to the process of industrialization. Historians have traced the elements of the Industrial Revolution back centuries into the Middle Ages (Pirenne 1937; White 1962). Viewed from this perspective there has been a continuous, small, evolutionary change, but not a revolution. However from the middle of the eighteenth century on, the rate of change in material technology has become so rapid as to periodically overturn the power and position of whole occupations and classes of society. Thus, the term "revolution" is not an overstatement, for, as Barrington Moore (1966) has shown, a genuine revolution need not be associated with short term cataclysmic political and military events. Summarizing the English revolution of the seventeenth century which cleared the way for rapid industrialization he says (1966:29), "that the violence and coercion which produced these results took place over a long space of time, that it took place mainly within a framework of law and order helped ultimately to establish democracy on a firmer footing, must not blind us to the fact that it was massive violence exercised by the upper classes against the lower."

In order to see this revolutionary potential for all aspects of society, we turn first to examine the early stage of industrialization in England. We will find in this early stage many problems parallel to those we face today in the emerging era of automation.

Early Industrialization

Numerous scholarly books have traced the causes of the Industrial Revolution, but this is not our purpose. We will look at six specific aspects of this revolutionary process in order to explicate further the multiple links between technology, social structure, and values. Each of the six illustrations deals with one aspect of the political system as well.

The Social Technology of Commercial Agriculture and Political Development

While the Industrial Revolution centrally involved the production of goods by machinery in factories, it was given great impetus by changes taking place in agricultural production during the seventeenth and eighteenth centuries. An examination of the development of commercial agriculture by

the landed aristocracy will afford us an opportunity to illustrate the ramifying consequences of these changes in technology, particularly in shaping
political institutions. This section is drawn primarily from Barrington Moore's
*Social Origins of Dictatorship and Democracy: Lord and Peasant in the
Making of the Modern World.* His is a highly complex analysis, and the
present discussion only traces one aspect in an oversimplified form. His full
discussion does not have the ring of technological determinism implicit in
this bare outline.

In feudal times land was, by and large, the basis of temporal power,
though it was not sought for the income it could produce. Rather, land
was valuable to the nobility insofar as it could support men, horses, and
the paraphernalia of feudal warfare. To maintain its political autonomy,
each estate was, as much as possible, economically self-sufficient. Thus, in
a very direct way, the end product of agricultural production was war-
making potential.

With the increasing pacification of the countryside by royal armies
there was no need for each estate to maintain a garrison. With the elaboration of civil law and royal police forces sufficient to make the law effective,
regular commerce became possible. The landed gentry increasingly turned
to producing agricultural products best suited to their land, exchanging these
goods in the developing towns for cash and the other goods they required.
In this context, land became valued for the income it could produce rather
than for the garrison it could support. Thus, a market economy in the products of commercial agriculture developed rapidly.

Some forms of commercial agriculture required more, and some fewer,
workers than were normally supported by the garrison estates. In the former
case, the landed gentry reinforced the feudal bonds that tied their peasants
to the land in order to guarantee sufficient labor for the emerging commercial farming; in the latter, the gentry sought means of abrogating their
feudal obligations to the unwanted peasants and began to move them off
the land.

Moore's Thesis. With these developments in mind, it is now possible
to present briefly Moore's argument. He asserts that factors of geography,
climate, and market determine the crop which becomes the basis for commercial agriculture in a given nation or region. The nature of the technology
required to produce the crop determined whether the landed gentry needed
more or less labor; this in turn makes for specific political and legal arrangements between the social strata, either binding the peasants to the land or
expropriating the peasants' land. Moore argues that these differing arrangements crystallized and became rationalized as three distinct ideologies—
democracy, fascism, and communism. What is more, these contrasting ideological commitments have become institutionalized and have remained
long after commercial agriculture has ceased to be of great importance to
the national economies in question.

Democracy. Moore illustrates this thesis by tracing the development of commercial agriculture in a number of nations. In England, the most important form of commercial agriculture was sheep which were produced for their wool. By the process of "enclosure" the landed aristocracy drove the peasant subsistence farmers off the land and converted it into pasture. The plight of the peasant is neatly caught in the seventeenth century phrase, "sheep eat men." While they were divesting the peasants of the land traditionally used by all community members, the aristocracy altered the Poor Laws, freeing themselves of the feudal obligation of caring for the dispossessed people on their estates. The ideology developed to rationalize this expropriation involves the notions of equality and freedom, fundamental to the later notions of liberal democracy.

Wine production was the prime form of commercial agriculture in much of France. It required great amounts of relatively skilled labor. Before the French Revolution, peasants ran the estates while the aristocratic owners, living at the royal court, contented themselves with taking rent off the land. These wine producing peasants strongly backed the early phases of the French Revolution, in order to divest the aristocracy of title to the land. This accomplished, they became a conservative force, checking the aspirations of industrial workers.

For the American case, Moore contrasts the multi-crop family farm of the Midwest with the single crop cotton or tobacco plantation based on slavery in the South. He sees the Civil War as, in large part, a contest over whether the federal government would serve the interest of one or the other of these two opposed forms of commercial agriculture. The outcome was a triumph for free labor, equality, and industrialization over caste and aristocratic agrarianism. Moore sketches another possible outcome which would have radically changed the course of later political events in the United States. Had Southern cotton been shipped to Northern mills rather than to England, had there been greater labor unrest in Northern factories, and had Midwestern farmers not been so politically powerful, an alliance might have been formed between the aristocratic Southern planters and Northern industrialists to check and control the slave and industrial workers' demand for freedom. The outcome of this alliance might well have been a political system much like that of fascist Germany.

Fascism. The relationship between lord and peasant in Germany and Japan contrasts with the three cases just discussed. The landed aristocracy of Germany and Japan built their commercial agriculture on crops requiring intensive labor practices—the one in wheat and rye, the other in rice. Both retained close managerial control over production and perpetuated or reinstated feudal laws binding peasants to the land. While their peasants were not literally chattel that could be bought and sold, they were legally required to work on a given estate and were thus an asset to be considered when assessing the worth of a piece of property. In both these nations the agrarian elite combined with the rising industrialists to thwart the drive for independence among farm and industrial workers. A prime outcome of this political alliance was industrialization managed through a strong national government by a small aristocratic elite. In both countries, this *managed* industrialization was rationalized through the ideology of fascist nationalism.

Communism. Another class of cases which Moore discusses involves peasant rebellion; his prime example is China. Here the landed elite did not develop commercial agriculture to any great degree, and industrialization has gone forward under communist leadership only *after* a massive peasant rebellion and continuous foreign invasion before and during World War II. Moore draws a tentative parallel between China and the industrialization under communism in the USSR. These go beyond our present interest except to note, as he makes clear, that in each of the seven instances discussed the early stages of industrialization have involved exploitation, turmoil, and often open warfare. Unfortunately, the predictions of early social theorists such as Saint-Simon, Spencer, and others that industrialization would bring an end to endemic warfare have not proved correct—at least in the first century and-a-half of the process. In any case the assertion at the heart of Moore's argument, that the different sorts of technology of commercial agriculture could influence the course of political development along democratic, fascist, or communist lines, dramatically illustrates the impact of the mode of technology on developing political institutions.

THE FLEECING OF WOOL: AN EXAMPLE OF LEGISLATIVE PLANNING

Among the English social planners of 1700, in the government and out, there was little doubt that "the prosperity of the country was chiefly maintained by the woolen industry" (Mantoux 1961:49). This industry was dispersed throughout the United Kingdom, employed more common people than any other, was a prime source of income for the landed aristocrats that controlled the House of Commons, and was a major item of foreign trade, bringing wealth both to merchants and the royal treasury. Thus, it served the interest of commerce, lords, and crown alike to maintain wool production and manufacture as a favored industry. This favored position led both to the protection and the tight control of the industry by diverse acts of Parliament. These government actions intended to favor the wool interest in fact facilitated the development of cotton manufacture. In examining this ironic development we will have a chance to see the influence of political action on the development of technology.

The wool industry was protected in many ways. For example, in the eighteenth century it was the law of the land for everyone to be buried in a suit of wool. This stipulation was rationalized on grounds of hygiene, but its most obvious effect was to augment the consumption of wool. In the late seventeenth century the British East India Company began to import quantities of cotton goods from India. The Madras prints and calicoes, being exotic, light, colorful, and soft, became the height of fashion. This led to widespread unemployment among wool weavers. People wearing cotton clothes were attacked and had their clothes burned by wool workers; stores selling cotton goods were sacked and their proprietors discredited. In 1700 Parliament responded to this popular violence by passing an act forbidding the importation of printed fabrics from Asia. Apparently enforcement of this act was lax, for the agitation was renewed and a more explicit law was passed in 1721. This act states clearly its own rationale:

> ...it is most evident that the weaving and using of printed, painted, stained, and dyed calicoes in apparel, household stuff, furniture and otherwise, does manifestly tend to the great detriment of the woolen and silk manufactures of this Kingdom, and to the excessive increase of the poor, and, if not effectively prevented, may be the utter ruin and destruction of the said manufactures, and of many thousands of Your Majesty's subjects and their families, whose livelihood does entirely depend thereon. (Mantoux 1961:200)

These anticotton laws, if successfully enforced, should have driven cotton products from England. But, something quite different happened, for the prohibition against importation, together with a lively demand for cotton products, stimulated the rapid expansion of cotton manufacture in England itself. Actually, the manufacture of cotton goods in England had begun on a small scale about 1691. The product was far inferior to the Indian stuff, but, when importation was curtailed, the industry began to flourish due to a continuing great popular demand. The wool weavers attacked this new rival with articulate ideological invective, as is evidenced by the small pamphlet entitled *The Just Complaints of the Poor Wool Weaver Truly Represented*. It states in part:

> As if the Nation was never to want a set of men to undo her, no sooner were the East Indian Chintz and printed calicoes prohibited from abroad, but some of Britain's unnatural children set all their arts to work, to evade the law of prohibition, to employ people to mimic the more ingenious Indian, and to legitimate the grievance by making it a manufacture here. (Mantoux, 1961:203)

These British cotton manufacturers evaded the letter of the law by mixing linen with cotton, dying rather than printing designs on the cloth, and similar tactics. In addition, they began to import the raw cotton not from Asia but from the West Indies. The crown was loathe to stop this traffic because it had a direct financial interest in the profitableness of the Caribbean cotton plantations. Thus, in a sincere effort to preserve the woolen industry, Parliament actually protected the English cotton industry in its first stages of development.

The tradition of government control of all aspects of manufacture in the woolen industry had grown out of the medieval customs intended to protect all elements of the industry, farmers, craftsmen, merchants, and customers alike, but the controls aided the growth of the rival cotton industry. While woolen manufacturers were rigidly controlled by statute, manufacturing custom, and craft guild prerogatives, the new English cotton manufacturers were free to experiment with new machines and new methods of organizing work such as gathering workers into factories. They took great advantage of the insatiable market for cotton goods and freedom from traditional regulations to experiment freely, as we will show in the next section.

THE MOTHERS OF INVENTION: TINKERING TO SCIENCE

The first English cotton manufacturers adopted the "putting-out" system of social technology, then prevalent in the production of woolen goods. Both spinning and weaving were performed with simple hand equipment in the laborer's home. From the introduction of the "flying shuttle" in 1733 to the first application of the steam engine to drive power looms and spinning machines in 1785, there was a veritable burst of invention which transformed this industry and became the model for industrialization in general (Mantoux 1961:200–209, 332–36; Smelser 1959:50–157).

This was an age intoxicated with the possibility that by tinkering with some machine in the productive process one could greatly expand productivity and turn a great profit. This urge to invent was justified as a means of learning God's laws, saving workers from the drudgery of hard menial labor, and strengthening English manufacturing against foreign competition. Thus religion, altruism, and patriotism were ideologically invoked to justify the continual disruption of production techniques. Such elaborate ideological rationalization of technological change was necessary in a society which still viewed work as properly bound in the traditional relation of hand production within the guild system (Bendix 1956:73–85).

Looking back, one can trace a sequence of inventions to present a picture of steady progress, but the *reality* was often quite different (Smelser 1959); the application of steam power to drive machinery provides an excellent case in point. The early heavy machines were driven by water power. Within a few years all convenient water falls and rapids in the relatively flat English countryside were harnessed. Since primitive steam pumps had already been developed to drain the water out of coal mines, it seemed a logical extension of this principle to pump water into huge tanks and drive machinery by harnessing the water falling from these reservoirs. Needless to say, this technique was extremely inefficient. Simple as it seems now to us, it took an act of genius to link the steam engine directly to machinery without going through the wasteful intermediate step of converting steam power to water power before applying the power directly to the machinery (Mantoux 1961:311–20).

Out of the trial and error process a new method of searching for improvements emerged, which relied less on tinkering and more on developing abstract principles applicable in a wide range of situations. What is more, this rational, scientific, and reform orientation gradually spread beyond the work place to all other aspects of life (Bendix 1956:73–89). But the role of inventor was replete with hazards nonetheless; while it was possible to obtain patents to protect the rights to use inventions providing a tremendous money incentive to inventive tinkering, patents were often infringed upon or stolen. Much time and money were expended in legal action; and, in at least one instance, the inventor who gained a patent and drew up contracts with entrepreneurs eager to use his machine was attacked by the workers to be displaced by his invention. He was literally driven out of England by their wrath with the willing support of the entrepreneurs who then had to pay no royalties for the use of his invention (Mantoux 1961:234–38, 399–408).

WAGE SLAVERY AND SOCIAL REFORM

A prime product of the factory system was a new sort of man—the wage worker. Neither was he a slave or peasant, nor was he a property owner or independent craftsman. He fit into none of these clearly differentiated roles of feudal society, yet, hundreds of thousands of these men peopled the industrial towns of England. Marx and Engels termed him the "wage slave":

> A class of laborers, who live only so long as they find work, and who find work only so long as their labor increases capital. These laborers, who must sell themselves piecemeal, are a commodity, like every other article of commerce, and are consequently exposed to all the vicissitudes of competition, to all the fluctuations of the market (Marx and Engels 1848:16).

To men used to tilling land or being employed in small shops the confinement, heat, noise, dust, long hours, physical danger, and strenuous involvement of only a small set of muscles was very nearly intolerable. Even more galling was the experience of being tied to the rapid, unchanging pace of the machine under the close and often brutal supervision of overseers who were paid on the basis of the amount of work they extracted from those in their charge. In many instances, workers likened the factory to a prison. Thus, factory work was universally loathed by workers.

As a result, the first generations of industrial manufacturers found real difficulty in recruiting a labor force which willingly sought factory work. Those who did come were most often peasants driven from the land by the Acts of Enclosure, Irish and Welsh men driven by starvation, and persons taken on contract from the poorhouse and orphanage. Parents sometimes bound their children to mill owners for a fee under the *guise* of apprenticeship, but, since no useful craft was taught, this apprenticeship differed little from chattel slavery. Consequently, local regulations regarding the poor were vigorously enforced to gain more persons to be indentured to the mill owners. Some municipalities bargained, so that owners would have to take one idiot for every twenty able-bodied paupers or children (Mantoux 1961:408–14)!

The work hours in these early factories were fantastic; to be sure, in Roman times, workers put in long hours, but one third of all days of the year were set aside as festival days. In medieval times, many Saint's Days were observed, and the hours of work were geared to the variable needs of agriculture. Medieval craftsmen had, according to one well documented record, 141 Saint's Days off *plus* a thirty-day vacation. Over the course of a year, these men worked 2,328 hours. By 1750 the number of hours worked in factories had risen to 3,770, and the number of hours hit a peak of 4,200 a year—nearly sixteen hours a day—about 1800! Today by comparison, annual work hours for factory workers is down to the range of 1900 to 2400 hours—a return to the prefactory level (Wilensky 1961:33–35).

Testimony. The wretched working conditions can be glimpsed from testimony given before parliamentary commissions of inquiry into textile mills made in 1832 and the coal mines in 1842.

Testimony of Mr. Matthew Crabtree (Bowdich and Ramsland 1961: 84–85).

At what age did you first go to work in a factory?
Eight.
Will you state the hours of labor at the period when you first went to the factory in ordinary time?
From six in the morning to eight at night.
Fourteen hours?
Yes. I have seen some overseers encouraging children to sing hymns in order to keep awake; others would be beating them about, and throwing things at them to keep them awake.
During those long hours of labor, could you be punctual; how did you wake?
I seldom did awake spontaneously; I was most generally awoke or lifted out of bed, sometimes asleep, by my parents.
Were you always on time?
No.
What was the consequence if you had been too late?
I was most commonly beaten.
Severely?
Yes, severely. I was, when working those long hours commonly much fatigued at night, when I left my work; so much so that I sometimes should have slept as I walked if I had not stumbled and started awake again; and so

sick often that I could not eat, and what I did eat I vomited. All that we
did when we got home was to get a little bit of supper that was provided for
us and to go to bed immediately. If the supper had not been ready directly,
we should have gone to sleep while it was preparing. I generally was beaten
when I happened to be too late, and when I got up in the morning the
apprehension of that was so great, that I used to run, and cry all the way
as I went to the mill.

Testimony of Joshua Drake (Bowdich and Ramsland 1961: 82–83),
concerning the work of his daughter who died of pulmonary complications
at age 14.

Was she a healthy girl?
She was very healthy when she went there.
Was it the dust that injured her health?
Whether it was the dust, or being sometimes over-worked til she sweated
and then chilled again, I cannot say. But I think that of the four girls that
were her comrades, three of them are dead.

Testimony gathered by the Mines Commission of 1842.
The following testimony was taken from girls employed in the mines
as "hurriers"—that is, children who pushed or pulled small carts of coal
to the surface on their hands and knees through the cramped, dank veins.
Testimony of Patience Kershaw (Bowdich and Ramsland 1961:89–90).

I wear a belt and chain in the workings to get the carts out. The coal leaders
I work for are naked except their caps; they pull off all their clothes; sometimes they beat me, if I am not quick enough, with their hands; they strike
me upon my back; the boys take liberties with me, sometimes, they pull me
about; there are about twenty boys and fifteen men; all men are naked, I
would rather work in the mills than in the coalpits.

Testimony of Ann Eggley (Bowdich and Ramsland 1961:87), age 18.

I began to hurry when I was seven and I have been hurrying ever since.
We wear trousers and our shifts in the pits and great big shoes clinkered
and nailed. The girls never work naked to the waist in our pit. The men
don't insult us in the pit. The conduct of the girls in the pit is good
enough sometime and sometimes bad enough. I never went to day-school.
I went a little to Sunday school, but I soon gave it up as I thought it too
bad to be confined both Sundays and weekdays. I have never learned to
read, I don't know my letters, I have never learned naught.

Apparently, the conditions just described were not unusual. Mantoux
(1961:414), for example, notes that strict protections were required to
prevent mass suicides among the poorhouse child laborers. The first reported
cases of "factory fever" broke out near Manchester in 1784. This bundle of
symptoms bred on malnutrition, dampness, heat, cold, dust, and fatigue was
soon diagnosed in widely scattered industrial districts, and was responsible
for many deaths (Mantoux 1961:415). With most family members employed twelve to eighteen hours a day and receiving subsistence wages, it is

not surprising that the extrawork life of laborers was nearly bestial (Cole and Postgate 1961:190–250; Kuczynski 1967:39–78). In fact the contrast in life styles between wage workers and the middle classes was then quite as wide as it is now between ghetto dwellers and middle class suburbanites.

The deplorable conditions of factory workers and their families were brought to the attention of the upper classes by the parliamentary commissions and the writings of men such as Charles Dickens; but at the same time, the masses were most often seen in their squalor and in their sporadic violence. Thus, the upper classes were filled with strong but ambivalent feelings of guilt and fear for the emerging new class. Feelings that humans should not be treated in this degrading way were mixed with the suspicion that they formed a species, a class, an element which could never be integrated into English civil society. Irish Catholic immigrants, for example, were perceived by many to be as different from white, Protestant Anglo-Saxons as contemporary white racists perceive blacks. At the same time, as Mantoux notes: "To the Puritan mind, the factory, with its mixture of depravity and suffering, of barbarity and vice, offered a perfect picture of hell" (Mantoux 1961:416). The question, then as now, is—to what extent is the condition of the lower classes a necessary product of machine technology; and to what extent is their plight a product of a social technology and a social structure which could be modified while retaining the fruits of industrial technology?

MACHINE-BREAKING, REPRESSION, AND POLITICAL REFORM

The emerging industrial working class did not simply submit to its dismal fate. In fact, between 1760 and 1842 there were a number of local peasant and town worker mob insurrections. Some were bread riots in times of famine, a few were primarily political uprisings on the pattern of the French Revolution, but many focused on the destruction of industrial machinery (Mantoux 1961:401; Thompson 1963:547–602; Smelser 1959: 357). At the forefront of the machine-breakers were those who had been technologically displaced by the new machinery, such as the hand loom craftsmen. Looking back, these were quite small, local, and ineffectual affairs, but, in contemporary perspective, they were most alarming to the upper classes.

The reaction of the government and other elements of the establishment was quite ambivalent. On the one hand, the government used troops and deployed cannon to dispel crowds; it outlawed union organization, and infiltrated the secret societies which workers had developed in the new industrial towns; and it regularly deported to Australia leaders of the agitation or simply executed them. On the other hand, Parliament passed a number of laws in an effort to reinstate the protections which workers had enjoyed in the medieval craft guild days. These laws were, in practice, unenforceable because of the new realities of factory production. In addition, the government greatly increased welfare payments and manipulated the Corn Laws in an effort to stabilize the price of bread. These actions were taken to alleviate widespread starvation and forestall agitation (Thompson 1963:315–18; Hobsbaun 1959; Smelser 1959).

The government's mixed strategy of repression and reform was successful in bringing about gradual change without provoking, in England, a general rising, parallel to the French Revolution. But, in the 1820s, the government could not help but project into the future a rising level of agitation and its policies were at a crossroads (Silver 1966). It could greatly enlarge the regular army and deploy it to the many, scattered industrial towns. But, such a strategy of forceful reaction would have required a large number of local garrisons, because in this era before rail, truck, and air transport, riot troops could not quickly be deployed. Alternatively, the establishment could accede to a number of reforms in voting rights, religious toleration for Catholics, welfare, labor law, tariff, and civil rights, which, when taken together, would begin to incorporate the newly rising industrial working class into the fabric of English civil life and to regularize the mediation of their grievances through normal political and legal channels.

Establishment Ambivalence. Most elements of the ruling class were afraid of taking this latter course, for workers were considered an inferior race incapable of playing a responsible political role, yet the alternative was full of dangers as well. The regular army was dispersed throughout the far-flung empire; in 1826 only four of the eighty-three regular army regiments were stationed in England. To call more home would endanger the empire's commitments which were increasingly important to the commercial and economic life of the mother country. To expand greatly the regular army was thought a prohibitive expense as well as a very real political danger, for the military might take over the government (Silver 1966). To rely on local militia might prove a danger, for local troops might not shoot at their fellows, but instead turn on their officers, thus triggering a general rebellion as in Paris; or, where the militia was commanded by the manufacturers, it might be used to enforce work in the mills.

Thus, in the face of the high economic and political cost of repression, the establishment reluctantly and haltingly embraced the task of incorporating the emerging industrial working class into British civil society (Silver 1966; Sterns 1967; Smelser 1959:384–401; Thompson 1963). The parallel between this case and that of contemporary ghetto blacks and, indeed, of the urban poor around the world is perhaps instructive. Let us hope that the relatively improved technologies of troop movement and riot control do not tempt governments to opt for repression over emancipation in the years ahead.

Two Strategies of Constructing Working-Class Social
Structure

Many theories developed about this new class which, to use Marx's
cryptic phrase, "had nothing to lose [by revolution] but its chains." Most
leading economists argued from their "laws" of economics and demography
that factory wages could be, in the long run, no higher than the biological
subsistence level. In its crudest form, the notion was that if wages rose
above that level, the lower classes would simply breed more future laborers,
thus depressing wages. Within this perspective all forms of social welfare
were foredoomed because they would increase the population and consequently impoverish the nation by increasing the welfare burden. The classic
statement of this stance is to be found in *An Essay on the Principle of
Population* by Thomas Malthus, written in 1798. One of the most perceptive
of the early political economists, John Stuart Mill (1848:365–66), pro-
pounded a policy which has a very contemporary ring in asserting that it
would be possible for the government to guarantee employment at ample
wages to all those who are born if no person were born without the government's consent. This wish for high wages and population control, which
is so near our reach, was quite utopian in 1848 when he wrote.

Paternalism. In practice two general strategies of incorporating the
new industrial men into civic society evolved: "paternalism" and "fraternalism," which continue to be applied (in modified form) even today; therefore, they deserve our attention. Paternalism was first systematically put into
practice by Robert Owen in his own mills, and was widely copied by other
early manufacturers. Owen bought a mill in the countryside and provided
cottages for his workers; he built schools, churches, stores; he provided a
police force and town government; he cut the hours of work and guaranteed,
as far as possible, regular employment. By providing these extrawork facilities and services, he developed a healthy, sober, loyal, trained, pious, and
docile work force. To further motivate workers, he kept a daily record of
the productivity and conduct of each worker and posted this record con-
spicuously. He saw himself as a *father* to his large family of workers (Bendix
1956:49–52; Cole and Postgate 1961:215–19; Mantoux 1961:467–68;
Smelser 1959:253–56).

By its advocates, paternalism was likened to the lord-serf relationship
of Feudalism, but in that system the action of a lord was circumscribed by
custom, so that he was bound to his serfs nearly as much as they were to
him. Free of any tradition, however, the *industrial* paternalist could be
much more arbitrary in his actions (Knox 1955:109–15). Not only were
hours and conditions of work less circumscribed by tradition, but the
paternalist could also profit from renting cottages and operating the community grocery store. The school could train manual arts and discipline,

the church could preach a love of authority, docility, and hard work, while the police could become spies, screening new workers and rooting out malcontents.

All these exploitative practices and more were employed by later paternalists (Lindsey 1943; Buder 1968; Uphoff 1966; Pope 1965), but, in the early stage of industrialization, the paternalistic factory-town was a creative and facile solution to the problem of transforming uprooted peasants into an urban laboring class (Moore 1951). It stands as a kind of half-way house between the Middle Ages and modern industrial society in that the *form* of labor-management relations was in the old pattern while its *content* was in the new.

Fraternalism. The alternative pattern to paternalism is *fraternalism.* The relationship between owner and workers is purely an exchange of work for wages, and the entrepreneur assumes no direct responsibility for workers outside of working hours. In this context, the worker is left to develop his own way of life with his peers.

Workmen gathered in ale houses and pubs and over the years, these places of congregation provided much more than alcoholic relief from the satanic mill. They spawned a wide range of working-class organizations, including labor unions, political clubs, burial societies, savings banks, consumer cooperatives, self-improvement societies, and recreational clubs. They were thus a most surprising source of social invention (Bendix 1956:86–99; Smelser 1959:343–83).

At the same time, elements of the middle class, appalled by the degrading conditions they saw around factories, began philanthropic efforts and financed Methodism, a new church established to meet the emotional needs of the working masses who were alienated from the established Anglican Church (Bendix 1956:60–73). While their motivation was often paternalistic humanitarianism, they brought the rudiments of education, dietetics, and hygiene to the poor.

When fully developed, the working-class fraternalism was a stable, largely self-regulating, and humane community (Blumer 1960; Bendix 1961; Smelser 1959:342–83; Mantoux 1961:440–77). The best case study of this way of life, readily available to the general reader, is to be found in the "Middletown" of 1880–1890, which Robert and Helen Lynd (1929) contrast with the conditions of blue collar workers at the time of their study in the mid 1920s.

Technology and Social Structure. While paternalism and fraternalism developed in the same era, their development in one industry or another probably was not a random happenstance, but rather was conditioned by the machine technology of the industry. This conjecture has never been thoroughly researched, but I suspect that paternalism was the predominate pattern in *machine-tending* technologies such as in the textile industry, which required primarily a mass of unskilled workers (Peterson and Demerath 1965). By contrast fraternalism developed where *craft factory* production was the prime technology (Freudenberger and Redlich 1964). In such cases, the crucial operations required the attention of skilled craftsmen, augmented by some heavy machines and a number of less skilled, younger workers. Such craft production was the technology in the glass jar factories of Middletown prior to the introduction of machines which mechanically blow glass on an assembly line basis (Lynd and Lynd 1929).

Machine-tending technologies, such as those in the textile industry, have continually been updated but not radically changed, right up to the emerging era of automation (Fensham and Hooper 1964). By contrast, craft factory technologies have often been radically altered by the introduction of *mass production* techniques in the early part of this century (Warner and Low 1947). It is to this technological transformation which we now turn.

Chapter **3**

CONTEMPORARY
TECHNOLOGIES

While many industries were still only just beginning to feel the impact of mechanization, several others began to undergo changes in machine and social technology far more complex than anything that could be encompassed within machine-tending or craft factory production. This next phase of the Industrial Revolution has been called *mass production*. It has spread widely, and is only now beginning to be supplanted in some industries by *automation*. The technologies of mass production and automation and some of their links to ideology and social structure form the subject of this chapter.

Mass Production

Just as the cotton textile industry was the leading industry in the earliest phases of the Industrial Revolution, the transcontinental railroad led the way in the second half of the nineteenth century; and the automobile, produced on a moving assembly line, led in the first half of this century. This is not to say that the new inventions involved in mass production were *first* applied in these industries or that *all* other industries followed their lead in converting to mass production (Blauner 1964:6–10), but simply that these industries exhibited what was new on a broad scale, profoundly influencing the technological and social practices of their time (Rostow 1962:55). In shifting our focus from cotton to rails and autos, we move from England to the United States, because it is here that the new technologies first had their impact. The first three sections of this part of the chapter deal with the social technology of mass production; the next section shows some of its effects on technology and social structure; and the final section deals with its machine technology.

SOLVING THE PROBLEM OF COORDINATION

While the early phases of industrialization dealt primarily with the application of power to the production process, as Faunce (1965) notes, the next phase with which we are concerned here, involved the mechanization of materials-handling techniques. Faunce's model of this change in machine technology is the transformation of auto making from machine shop to assembly lines mass production, but an analogous change in *social* technology was necessary to coordinate thousands of people employed in diverse tasks in widely separated areas. The social invention which was perfected to solve the problems of coordination is called *bureaucracy*. The principles of bureaucratic coordination were developed and perfected not in industry but in the massive standing armies and far-flung railroads of the nineteenth century a full generation before it was applied to industry. Military and railroad organizers freely borrowed techniques from each other in this development particularly in Germany, where industry and military were coordinated through a strong nationalistic central government (Moore 1966; Jacob 1963; Bendix 1956).

Bureaucracy can quite fairly be seen as a technique for materials handling *if* the concept is broadened to include the transfer of *information* within a system. Both assembly line production and bureaucratic coordination are answers to the demand for the mass production of relatively sophisticated goods, services, and information; both also rely on a deliberate, systematic, and objective application of scientific and engineering procedures in the place of traditional craft skills and customary managerial practices; they both supplant the craft skills of the earlier industrial worker as well as the entrepreneurial innovativeness of the old owner-manager, as we shall see.

BUREAUCRACY AS SOCIAL TECHNOLOGY

In 1803 the first steam driven locomotive ran on iron rails. In 1830 the first *practical* railroad was opened, covering a distance of 30 miles between Liverpool and Newcastle, England. Only a decade later, all Eastern United States cities had short railroads poking into their immediate hinterland. In two more decades, New York and Chicago were connected, and on the eve of the Civil War two transcontinental railroads were chartered (Stover 1961).

This was an explosive rate of growth by any standards then known and created many problems for which answers were not readily available. As the rail lines expanded and ever more lines were interconnected, the logistics and scheduling of passengers and freight, as well as the increasing threat of collisions, created an acute problem of coordination. The rapid expansion of the industry also meant that there were not enough men trained for the diverse, complex new tasks at hand.

The answer to these problems of coordination was found in the development of standarized rules and procedures which defined the duties of each job, the scope of discretion its incumbent could wield, and the chain of command through which orders and questions could be channeled. These elements are foremost in Max Weber's (1947) classic definition of bureaucracy. This complex social machine, which spread over the entire nation along slim ribbons of steel, operated with great accuracy. Order was brought with a rule book, train schedule, table of traffic rates, and a gold pocket watch, even though the system was manned by sons of farmers with only a rudimentary reading skill.

Bureaucracy not only is a means of coordinating a complex set of routine tasks, it is also a principle of work *motivation*. To the list of elements just enumerated, Weber (1947) adds the following: appointment and promotion based on training and experience, payment by stated wages, and strict separation of the bureaucratic job from other aspects of life. In *each* of these particulars, the bureaucrat differs from the nineteenth century self-employed entrepreneur who was motivated to continuous hard work by risking his own money and time in an innovative venture; the bureaucrat is motivated by the expectation that following rules and procedures will guarantee a steady income and regular promotion.

Pathologies in Bureaucracy. While Weber stressed the rational aspects of bureaucracy, many contemporary researchers have shown the "irrationalities" inherent in bureaucracy. Three recurrent pathologies in bureaucracy will be cited. First, there is the problem that bureaucratic functionaries, rather than working to achieve the goals of the organization, will pay most attention to those aspects of their jobs which are most visible and for which they are rewarded by their supervisors. (This selective attention to part of the task is somewhat parallel to the case of those students who work for grades rather than an education.) This problem is easily diagnosed, but not easily cured, for a change in the basis of evaluation may simply lead to selective attention to the new criterion of evaluation (Blau 1955).

Second, the bureaucratic functionary may become so used to following rules that he is unable to adapt to new and changing situations. This sort of rule tropism has inspired generations of novelists to write of the orderly, dull, inhibited official who is the antithesis of the bohemian artist (Merton 1968:249–60; Mills 1953–233–38; Presthus 1962). On its most sinister side, this cathexis upon rules may become an ethic of irresponsibility.

It is so easy for the official, even the man operating the machines of human extermination, to say, "Don't blame me, I only follow orders" (Howton 1969).

Third, bureaucratic rules are generated to circumscribe the discretion and power of officials, but these officials may *use* the rules to help or frustrate other persons or groups who depend on them. Thus, "red tape" may be spun or cut at the discretion of bureaucratic functionaries to serve their own ends (Gouldner 1951; Mechanic 1962; Selznick 1952). This sort of possibility has recently come to national attention, as various workers have tried to enforce their wage demands, not by stopping work in the traditional fashion, but by following *all* the regulations which apply to their job to the letter of the law, thereby paralyzing complex activities such as the landing of aircraft at major airports.

Having pointed to three recurrent pathologies inherent in bureaucracy, it is probably still true that the low levels of technological education combined with the crude methods of information processing available before the advent of computers *did* make bureaucracy the most rational form of coordination in most industrial activities. We turn now to an examination of several industries which have not yet become bureaucratized.

WHERE BUREAUCRACY DOES NOT WORK

While many industries have organized or reorganized their social technologies along the bureaucratic lines tested on the railroads, others have not. By examining three such industries—printing, home building, and textiles—we can further understand the workings of bureaucracy and the link between social and machine technology.

Efforts at bureaucratization of the administration of production in the home-building industry have largely been resisted. Most houses are still built by numerous kinds of skilled craftsmen employed by independent contractors working without close supervision according to blueprints and general instructions. Their "professional" status contrasts markedly with bureaucratically administered auto assembly plants where workers are under the close supervision of foremen and work at a speed set by machines. Arthur Stinchcombe (1959), in noting the survival of craftsmen in home building, points to a number of characteristics of the industry which make it uneconomical to generate the technology of mass production and bureaucratic control in this industry. While he explains the survival of craft production as a consequence of factors inherent in machine technology, one might still ask whether industry custom, local building codes, and strong craft unions have not been equally important in maintaining craft production in this industry. The ever increasing production of mobile homes—the oversized descendants of the house trailer—and perfection of techniques for mass producing prefabricated house components are bitterly resisted by the traditional labor and management interests in the industry (Harwood 1971).

Printing is another industry which has long had a social technology of craft production (Lipset, Trow, and Coleman 1956), which has undergone rapid change over the past few years by the introduction of automated typesetting equipment (Loehwing 1968; Sulzo 1968; Lessing 1969). While there is an excellent study of the craft organization of the printing industry and the political implications of the craft order (Lipset, Trow, and Coleman 1956; Blauner 1964:35–67), there is no good sociological study of the consequences of the rapid automation for the worker both on the job and in the community.

Textiles, once the leading industry in technological development, has changed very little in the last hundred years. Reliance is still placed on masses of unskilled machine tenders. Technological change has been limited to modernizing old machines and procedures rather than to transforming the production process in ways comparable to the two industries just discussed (Fensham and Hooper 1964). In this industry, more than in almost any other, mills are still today located in company-dominated towns in which owners try to influence aspects of workers' lives in the classical pattern of paternalism (Peterson and Demerath 1965; Wall Street Journal Oct. 15, 1968). This pattern has been increasingly difficult to maintain since fraternalism has become so predominant. Over the last one hundred and fifty years, this industry has made a curious odyssey from England to New England, to the rural South, and now increasingly to underdeveloped countries. Whenever local labor becomes too sophisticated for paternalistic managers, plants have been moved farther from urban industrial areas in search of docile, unskilled, nonunion workers (Maxwell 1971). This affinity of machine-tending textile technology for paternalism is most impressive, as is that of the large scale produce farmers of California. Rather than moving to find docile labor, they have maintained paternalism by bringing wave upon wave of unsophisticated workers to the fields. Over the years these recruits have included the native Indians, Chinese, Japanese, Mexicans, Midwest Dust Bowl refugees, and most recently Philippinos (London and Anderson 1970:6–15).

You Can't Run a Railroad Within the Law

All of us know, from our exposure to American history, how railroad construction stimulated the steel industry and many others, how it stimulated the growth of cities, transformed uninhabited wastes into bountiful agricultural land, and bound together the vast continent. Few doubt that the railroad was indispensable to the industrialization and modernization of this nation (Rostow 1962). That it was also the leader in developing many modern business practices, both exemplary and corrupt, in its relations with the government, workers, mass media, and technological change makes it deserving of our attention here.

Government Financing. From its inception, the industry was dependent on local, state, and federal governments for capital, land grants, and other diverse privileges. Cochran and Miller (1961) cite the following figures. Federal cash grants to railroads came to over sixty-four million dollars during the last century and many small towns paid dearly to have a road built their way. For example, between 1867 and 1892, forty-three sparsely settled Nebraska counties had voted almost five million dollars to railroad companies, many of which never built a mile of track. The federal government alone ceded 200 million acres of land; in an investigation made in 1893 it was found that railroads had been granted one-fourth of the whole area of the states of Minnesota and Washington, one-fifth of Iowa, Kansas, North Dakota, Minnesota, and Wisconsin, as well as some of the best land in California and Lousiana!

Corporate Corruption. Railroad men spent freely for these grants. Between 1875 and 1885 according to its own records, the Union-Pacific Railroad alone paid over $500,000 annually in direct graft to legislators and government officials (Stover 1961). Huge private rail fortunes were made, not from service revenues for the use of the roads, but from the profits of dummy corporations created by the railroad owners. These men formed themselves into construction companies and voted themselves highly profitable contracts for building railroads and equipment; as directors of railroad companies they gladly paid the price that was asked. In addition, they sold large tracts of land to other dummy companies of their own, and these were resold at vastly higher prices to individual farmers and settlers, drawn west by extravagant promotional campaigns carried on by the railroads. In these ways public money was converted into private fortunes. While railroad executives became rich, their companies often went bankrupt (Cochran and Miller 1961).

This financial sleight of hand which was made possible by the creation of multiple interlinking companies is still a major strategy of respectable corporations. For example, Mutual Stock Investment Funds, which today handle the stock portfolios for tens of thousands of small investors, do not charge much for their *own services.* They do, however, hire stock market consulting companies at considerable expense to their subscribers; seeking "outside" expert advice seems prudent on the surface, but the fund managers are very often the sole owners of the consulting firms! So, in the name of receiving expert advice, Fund managers pay themselves well with the investors' money.

Shoddy Roadbuilding. Since the largest federal government land grants were given to the railroads on rail mileage completed, almost all of the roads were poorly constructed in an effort to outdistance rival lines.

Very quickly rails split, trestles collapsed, and whole sections of the railroads built through Western mountains had to be abandoned or completely rebuilt. In the final analysis, as Cochran and Miller (1961:135) note, it was not for their individual profiteering that these rail magnates should be most condemned, but for the fact that they built poor railroads. Much the same can be said of some parts of the interstate road system which have been built over the last ten years.

Like our contemporary highways, the railroad was a great cause of death and injury. As today, industry and public officials put the blame for this carnage on *human* error. As late as 1912 a commissioner of the Interstate Commerce Commission which was set up to regulate railroads said, "The most difficult and perplexing factor in this problem is the personal equation. The failure of the man at the critical moment is the thing to be guarded against" (Rice 1967:14). This statement was made in spite of the fact that economically feasible safety equipment, in existence for half a century, had not been fully deployed on the railroads.

Accurate figures for earlier years are not available, but between 1891 and 1895 there was an average of 6,000 deaths and 35,000 injuries on the roads each year, and as late as 1902, 2,600 employees and passengers were killed and 35,800 were hospitalized. By comparison, English and German railroads were quite safe (Rice 1967). It is instructive to review the factors which perpetuated the carnage in spite of the availability of safety technology, which included telegraphically linked automatic signal systems, air powered brakes, and automatic coupling devices.

In the early days the prime public concern was the extension of rail lines. In the 1880s newspapers found that train wrecks and "exorbitant" freight rates made great copy, and editorial attacks on rail "magnates" became popular. The roads responded by diverting large advertising revenues to the newspapers and liberally distributing free passes to newspaper men. In addition, they made a show of compensating dependents where spectacular train wrecks occurred (Stover 1961).

The Government Fosters Industry Cooperation. Quite often rival railroad companies could not agree upon a mutually beneficial solution to a common problem because no one company could unilaterally afford to make the change. In such instances, the government was asked to set standards. For example, in the 1850s the federal government intervened to establish a standard track gauge (the distance between the rails). Up to that time eleven different gauges had been widely used. Cars could not be switched from one line to another, so passengers and freight had continually to be unloaded and reloaded, thus increasing tremendously expense, inconvenience, and delays of all concerned.

The introduction of various devices to reduce the hazards of accidents to railroad workers provides another example of beneficial governmental intervention. Safety equipment was more expensive than conventional equipment and was not effective unless all carriers which interchanged cars adopted the same devices. The industry did not organize to initiate safety practices, so in the 1880s state legislatures moved to enforce the adoption of uniform safety equipment (Stover 1961).

In the area of industrial accident compensation, too, the government had to force the roads to develop accident insurance programs even though they actually lowered the cost of accidents to the railroad. The railroads resisted the plans as an interference in their affairs. In practice the medical insurance programs distributed more fairly the high damage costs which the railroads had formerly regularly incurred. Under the old system of individual damage claims, each accident involved not only the payment of medical expenses and damage fees, but also legal fees for court costs, all of which helped foster a negative public image of the railroads (Auerbach, Garrison, Hurst, and Mermin 1961:534–58). Thus we have here three illustrations of the emerging role of government in enforcing cooperation between corporations of an industry for their own good as well as that of the public when industry does not do so itself.

Pride Cometh Before a Fall. While management must bear most of the responsibility for the long delay in installing safety devices, labor probably contributed its part to the postponement. Many men would lose their jobs if air-brakes replaced the manual ones. The same thing applied to flagmen if automatic signals were adopted and if the automatic couplers were installed. Locomotive engineers fought the use of telegraphic signals to regulate trains as an interference with the independence and responsibility which they had traditionally enjoyed. In addition, workers regularly ignored those safety devices which slowed their work. For example, hundreds of men annually were crushed between cars in the act of manipulating old style pin-coupling devices because it was faster to the job by hand and it became a point of occupational pride not to use the safety device for positioning the pins.

Norms of craftsmanship and manliness grew up around aspects of the work process with surprising rapidity as we have just seen, and numerous examples can be drawn from contemporary work situations. For example, the large punch presses which stamp automobile body parts are built so that the operator must hold two separate switches to operate the press, thus insuring that his hands will not be crushed. Unions, insurance companies, and state governments have pressed for such devices. In practice, one of the switches is often taped down so that the operator can hold the metal until the last moment. Management says workers tape switches to show their bravery; operators say they can't meet their production quota without deactivating the safety devices. Of course, the corporation can enforce the use of safety devices, just as a decade ago construction companies pressured by insurance firms enforced the wearing of hard hats on construction jobs.

Workmen who at first thought these hats were for children and complained that they were clumsy and hot, now wear hard hats as a point of occupational pride and identification even when they are out of the way of danger (James 1969).

Sunk Costs Versus Technological Change. Numerous writers over the past fifty years have pointed to the reluctance of railroad men to adopt new advances in technology (Auerbach, Garrison, Hurst, and Mermin 1961; Rice 1967). They have generally explained this conservatism as a consequence of the fact that most railroad executives were trained in fiscal and not engineering habits of thinking; but there may be a more fundamental reason. Railroads, more than almost any other industry, have their capital invested in expensive and durable machinery and equipment. Such investments in plant and equipment are called "sunk" costs. What is more, most railroad equipment is part of a tightly interrelated system, so that new and old devices often cannot operate side by side, and any significant technological advance would mean scrapping massive amounts of sunk capital. I don't know of any research on this question, but I would advance the general hypothesis that the rate of adoption of new technologies is inversely related to the proportion of sunk capital characteristic of an industry.

In this section we have looked at problems caused by changing technology, both machine and social. While the railroad was a source of graft, corruption, price fixing, and injury, it also was the first industry to solve most of these problems. It was in railroading that the principles of accident insurance, labor law, corporation law, antitrust law, and the federal control of private industry by regulatory commission—all elements of the emerging close relationship between industry and government—were experimentally developed (Lindsey 1943; Auerbach, Garrison, Hurst, and Mermin 1961; Cochran and Miller 1961; Stover 1961; Eggert 1967; Rice 1967; Kerr 1968). While it is beyond the scope of this book, it would be instructive to compare the tumultuous development of railroads in America with their more stable and less problem-generating development in Germany and England.

MR. FORD'S ASSEMBLY LINE

As noted earlier, the era of mass production centrally involved the mechanization of materials-handling techniques. The automobile assembly line which was built by Henry Ford in 1909, although not the first, was the most singularly successful and the most widely copied example of this process.

As Henry Ford noted in his concise summary of the process in an article on "Mass Production" in the *Encyclopaedia Britannica* of 1939, "mass" refers not so much to the quantity of articles produced as the method of production. It relies on the simplification of work tasks in a carefully engineered matrix of sequential operations. Essential to this flow is the rigid *standardization* of parts fabricated without reference to the particular automobile into which the parts will finally be assembled. Now massive special purpose machines, operated by semiskilled workers, could be substituted for the array of general purpose machine shop tools operated by skilled craftsmen which had been required in the handcrafting of earlier automobiles.

Engineering the Job. As the engineers transformed the machinery of craft production into those of mass production it was understandable that they came to focus on the *worker* as an element of the *machine* system (Taylor 1911). Where the earlier manager assumed that the longer one worked the more he produced, the human engineers of scientific management made this an empirical question. With stop watch, notebook, and slide rule they found that fatigue, accidents, substandard production, absenteeism and labor turnover could be reduced by shortening work hours. Thus, another paradox was confirmed: A worker realizes more profit for the corporation if he is employed eight rather than ten or twelve hours a day (Gordon 1961).

These engineers observed human craftsmanship and analyzed it into numerous components. Wherever possible they recombined these components into machine operations and then instructed workers how best to operate the rebuilt machines and to perform the simplified tasks that remained. The human engineers managed in a few decades to decode the secrets of craftsmanship, learned over centuries, to create a technology requiring semiskilled operators with only a few days' training (Bell 1962; Bendix 1956; Walker and Guest 1952).

In mass production technologies, the pace of work is set largely by machines, and questions of productivity, profit, and quality depend on the speed of the assembly line. Today, the bare frame of a Lincoln Continental begins a quarter-mile trip at one-sixth m.p.h. (Rapoport 1967). There are 275 workers that attach components along the way. Each worker has about ninety seconds to complete his individual tasks. Just ninety minutes after it has begun this trip, the finished auto is driven off ready for final inspection and delivery. Fifteen inspectors and ten repairmen look for defects of assembly along the way, but at the high speed of the line, inspection cannot be thorough. As one inspector commented to the *Wall Street Journal* writer who was temporarily working on the assembly line, he only had time to check the trunk of each car closely enough to "make sure there is no dead foreman in there" (Rapoport 1967:1); thus, the primary difference in workmanship between a high priced and a standard American built automobile is the speed of the assembly line. Lincoln Continentals are paced at forty an hour, while standard Fords come off the line at sixty-five an hour. It is little wonder that in the first ten months of 1967 model car sales, more than a million American made autos were recalled from customers for suspected manufacturing defects (Nader 1967).

Mass Consumption. The necessary complement of mass production is mass consumption. Henry Ford could afford the elaborate technology and engineering costs of the assembly line only by volume production. To achieve this, he reduced the cost of his Model T from $900 in 1909 to $360 in 1914. This engineering strategy, geared to production as the first principle, contrasts markedly with the common strategy of earlier manufacturers who tried to corner markets and cut production to increase profits by raising prices. Ford saw his own workers as potential consumers and thus with great fanfare raised wages from $2.40 for a nine-hour work day to $5.00 for an eight-hour work day (Galbraith 1967). While Ford firmly believed in the apparent paradox that lowering prices and increasing wages would increase profits, he was able to put this theory into practice because of the tremendously high rate of profit the corporation realized throughout the period. Some have argued, however, that wages *had* to be increased to reduce the high rate of employee turnover on the assembly line jobs and to forestall labor union organization in the Ford plants. We will return to this question in Chapter 4.

Transformation of the Working Class Community. The impact of this breakdown of the skilled hierarchy was devastating to the working class family and community (Warner and Low 1947; Thernstrom 1965). While the craftsman could command good pay and respect based on his knowledge, and the young apprentice could look forward to a career of increasing knowledge, status, and pay, the mass production line reduced most workers to a semiskilled homogeneous mass. Rather than valuing experience gained with age, the assembly line valued the agility and strength of women and youth. Men faced rapidly deteriorating chances in the job market after the age of forty, and many fathers experienced the humiliation of being laid off in times of recession while their wives and children remained employed (Komarovsky 1940). The devastating impact on the working-class family and community has been poignantly chronicled in a number of sociological investigations (Lynd and Lynd 1937; Warner and Low 1947; Shostak 1969; Shostak and Gomberg 1964). These experiences radicalized many men during the first half of the present century and were the focal point of many strikes. The reasons these conditions did not lead to widespread political revolt against the new system will be explored in Chapter 5.

Automation

Here we are concerned with the emerging technological era of automation. While a few examples of automated machine technologies are now operational, its social technology is being implemented much more rapidly. Thus, social technology will receive relatively greater attention here than in the discussion of earlier technologies. Consideration of the effects of automation upon organizations, individuals, and society is deferred to the final three chapters of the book.

First, we must define this new but already much misused term "automation." Economic analysts tend to use the term "automation" to refer to *all* forms of contemporary technological change, because it is difficult to trace the effects of automation per se on income, employment, and profit. However, not all contemporary technological change involves the principles of automation, as we define them. The technological unemployment which has occurred in the coal mining industry since World War II, for example, is due to the mechanization of hand tool jobs and is thus comparable to the changes that took place in many other industries a generation or more ago. A *genuinely* automated coal mine might have pumps which would drive air into shafts drilled down into the earth to feed fires which would burn coal in the depth of the earth. The heat thus generated would be converted to electrical power, and the escaping gases could be processed to become a wide range of utilizable hydrocarbons or dyes, perfumes, and plastics. Such a coal mine is not yet in operation, but some of the ways of organizing work characteristic of automation already have been introduced into the backward coal industry. As in the case of each of the earlier stages of industrialization, social technology precedes machine technology and the consequences of these changes ramify well beyond the boundaries of industry. The effect of automation on social organization may be great, because it is not primarily a kind of machine, but, as we will show, a way of organizing machine and human processes that may be adopted by a Boy Scout troop or the Department of Defense, as well as by an industrial concern (Wiener 1966).

CYBERNATION

As noted earlier, the technological revolution has focused in turn on the application of power to machine production in textiles and the perfection of materials-handling techniques on the railroads and in automobile production. With automation, the *control* of the production process becomes mechanized (Faunce 1965). Thus automation involves the analysis of the *total* production process and the concomitant economic and social ramifications. The assembly and processing of the vast bodies of data needed for such analysis is made possible by the development of large, fast digital computers. In turn, computers largely perform the dull task of continually checking the system's performance and making the modifications necessary to obtain the desired results (Myers 1967).

The new *idea* that is at the heart of automation is called "cybernetics" (Wiener 1966). Cybernetics, or cybernation as it sometimes is called, is best understood by a comparison with the idea of mass production. Common to both the assembly line and bureaucracy is a *linear* sequence of steps *along* the line in the one case and *up* the hierarchy in the other. Such line organization is well adapted to routine operations but cannot easily meet changing circumstances. Cybernation does not replace the line; it builds onto the line a number of side loops. These connect points along the line to locate automatically and adjust for imperfections in the emerging product of the continuing process. Once the notion of a loop which feeds information back to modify earlier stages in the process is introduced, it is possible to develop ever more complex and intelligent machine systems (Dunlop 1962; Simon 1965; Forrester 1968). One of the best *models* of a cybernetic system is the human body in its metabolic processes. We are not soon likely to build automated systems with its cybernetic complexity, but this is the ultimate goal of every engineer (Stout 1962).

Objectification. The computer is often seen as the mark of automation. Certainly its speed of calculation and huge memory capacity are essential to the process. A more important requisite of automation in any industry is the exact specification of the criteria used in monitoring the production process. It has been easy to program computers to paint and compose music, because a *style* can be programmed, but computers have not been able to *judge* artistic work successfully; the genius of good art is that it *breaks* from established forms in ways that are neither programmed nor purely random.

This inability to objectify standards of measurement is currently one of the greatest hinderances to the more rapid spread of automation. Charles Silberman (1966:16) cites a telling example drawn from the basic oxygen process for smelting steel. System engineers wanted to construct a mathematical model to describe what actually goes on in the oxygen furnace. They found the available data too crude because the measuring instruments employed were not accurate enough. The crude data did not result from sloth on the part of steel engineers but from the fact that before computers were introduced they had no need for more refined data. Previously, steelmakers could rely on the pragmatic knowledge that the oxygen process worked and did not need to probe so deeply into why and how. Silberman concludes that it may well be easier to program a trip to the moon than to automate many of the more mundane industrial processes. While this may be true, he should add that unlike our venture into space, no one has seen fit to deploy tens of billions of dollars and the work of tens of thousands of scientists in automating steel production.

THE ADVENT OF AUTOMATION

For fifteen years magazines have told of whole factories that run themselves without the aid of workers. Such stories make gripping journalism, for the notion that man's inventions will arise to overcome him are probably as old as the species. But the current concern about automation is woefully wide of the truth. After studying illustrations given in published stories, Silberman (1966:2) concludes that "No fully automated process exists for any major product in any industry in the United States. Nor is any in prospect in the immediate future." Based on a careful analysis of the United States labor force, Faunce (1968:52) comes to much the same conclusion; by his relatively generous definition of automation, just 1.5 percent of all employed civilian workers are in industries having automated machine technologies.

While completely automated *machine* technologies are a thing of the future, the cybernetic logic of organizing work is already widely understood and is being put into practice. As in the case of mass production, it seems safe to predict that the social technology of automation will be widely implemented long before the machine technology of automation is a reality. While we do not make automobiles or war by automation, decisions about the procurement, deployment, and effectiveness of weapons systems, as well as analogous decisions in the auto industry, are now analyzed in cybernetic terms (Galbraith 1967; Wilensky 1967; Schon 1967).

Telephone Books: An Illustration. Both automobile and military cybernetic decision structures are permeated with political and personal considerations. A better illustration of cybernetic principles in practice is to be found in the manufacture of telephone directories. This sounds like prosaic business, the printing each year of a new directory. But the Bell Telephone Company management recently began to realize that directories are given out free at considerable cost to Bell. They asked, Why change each year? They found that as a directory becomes older, the number of requests for information, misdialed calls, and the like increase sharply, overloading available personnel and equipment. With the aid of a computer they found that in cities with high rates of mobility half the numbers in the book are obsolete within two years. Given the rate of turnover in telephone numbers, the available information equipment and personnel, the revenue from yellow page advertisements, and the cost of printing new books, the company can compute for each city how often to print new directories in order to minimize overall costs and maintain "adequate" service.

Telephone companies have always entrusted to printing concerns the task of producing directories on a city-by-city basis. This practice results in an annual cycle of feast and famine among printers and arouses intense competition between sectors of the telephone company to get their books produced on time. A staff group was organized to coordinate the printing tasks, but the coordination of production has now been taken over by systems engineers who have built a computer model which keeps in mind the press capacities of dozens of printing companies, the availability of paper stock, the capacity of electronic typesetters, and projected changes in book length. This cybernetic unit directs the procurement of printing contracts and continually updates its analysis over time in such a way that it "learns" from current experience.

THE CHANGING NATURE OF WORK

Between 1950 and 1967 United States industrial production *doubled* while the number of persons employed in production increased by only 12.6 percent (*Wall Street Journal* February 10, 1971). This means an increase of over 3 percent per year in worker productivity. Over the same period, total nonagricultural employment has expanded by 31.8 percent, mostly in professional, technical, white-collar, and service employments. But the jump in productivity and employment is *not* due to automation; according to Faunce's (1968:52) recent figures, only 1.5 percent of all workers currently work in advanced automated industries and an additional 4.5 percent are in industries which are beginning to automate. The number of workers directly affected by automation is further decreased by the fact that only part of the workers in these industries are in fact working in automated environments.

Thus it is difficult to use contemporary illustrations to understand what effects automation will have on employment, unemployment, and skill levels, for many contrasting projections have been made (Brozen 1963; Faunce 1968; Ryscavage 1967; Wolfbein 1962; Sultan and Prasow 1964). It seems safest to predict that automation will spread slowly and will transform some areas of work much more rapidly than others. Cybernetic technologies are most easily introduced into those industries which process fluids such as petroleum, plastics, chemicals, and the like (Blauner 1964; Meissner 1969). Such technologies may also be introduced into those aspects of other industries which can be treated as fluids—the flow of money, electrical power, goods, services, and information. The computer control of airline reservations is a good example of what is meant here. Reservation clerks can make, reconfirm, and cancel tickets on all major scheduled airlines while sitting at computer terminals located anywhere in the country. An index of the degree to which such information flows are already automated is the fact that over half of all telephone communication today involves computers "talking" to other computers. At the opposite extreme are individual services provided by psychiatrists and waiters in first-class restaurants which cannot be programmed readily.

Machine operators are rapidly replacing most day labor pick-and-shovel jobs and farm laborers. Above this level, however, it seems most likely that about the same distribution of blue-collar skills will be required for the rest of the twentieth century (Ryscavage 1967; Simon 1965). One consequence of automation will certainly be that the classical distinction between blue-collar factory work and white-collar office work will be rendered nearly meaningless (Siegman and Karsh 1962; Meyer 1968). Even today the production worker who monitors a bank of dials in the control room of an automated continuous process chemical plant has more responsibility, skill, and control over his work activities than the common office worker who operates an IBM tabulating machine or a Xerox copier (Mann and Hoffman 1960; Faunce, Hardin, and Jacobson 1962; Blauner 1964; Winter 1970: 28). Finally, automation will make possible the substitution of more flexible forms of organization for the relatively rigid bureaucratic forms of contemporary technologies (Simon 1965). We will return to this prospect in discussing emerging forms of organization in the next chapter.

SIZE AND COMPLEXITY MAKE PLANNING IMPERATIVE

Perhaps the most vital consequence of the organizational changes just outlined is that long-term systematic planning has become *imperative* (Klein 1971). A most telling example of the growth of this imperative comes from Galbraith who gives a description of the changing nature of the automobile industry, an account from which we freely borrow here (1967:11–21).

After several months of negotiations for capital and certain components, the Ford Motor Company was formed in June 1903. Stock worth $100,000 was issued, and 125 production workers were hired. In October, less than five months after the company was formed, the first auto reached the market and the company showed a profit before the end of the year.

Compare this first Ford with the introduction of the Ford Mustang in September 1964. Planning and preparation for the Mustang required three and one-half years; for the latter half of this time, there was a fairly firm commitment to the details of the car that eventually emerged. Careful studies of market potential and merchandizing techniques were performed, because the decision was to be backed by an investment of nine million dollars in engineering and styling costs and fifty million dollars in tooling up for production. Ford at this time averaged 317,000 employees and had assets of about six billion dollars.

The names of most of Henry Ford's early competitors are remembered only among antique car buffs. As entrepreneurs were not always successful, contemporary planners make errors as well. Ford's adventure with the Edsel in the late 1950s is a good example of planning gone astray (Long 1968a). The total cost of design, assembly, and promotion of the Edsel was a quarter of a *billion* dollars, and it was estimated that it would take approximately 200,000 auto sales to break even on this investment. The Edsel was introduced in September 1957, and just 35,000 were sold the first model year. When the last Edsel rolled off the assembly line in November 1959, 109,466 had been produced. The loss in production totaled 200 million dollars, making the total cost to Ford of 450 million dollars. A bit over 100 million dollars of this total would be recouped in reassigning plants and equipment, and through taxes.

Five Reasons For Planning. Based on the automobile examples, Galbraith (1967:13–15) notes five consequences of the changes in technology between Henry Ford's time and our own which make long-term systematic planning *imperative* for all those in the crucible of industry. The imperatives include first: an increasing span of time from design to finished product. As Galbraith notes, combat aircraft which saw extensive service in World War II had been substantially designed before the war. Today the time between conception and development of weapons systems is almost a decade. Second: there has been a tremendous increase in the capital expenditure necessary for a new venture. It took $100,000 for Ford to translate his ideas into an auto in 1903. In 1957 it took a quarter of a billion dollars! Third: commitments once made constrain future actions, thus greatly reducing organizational flexibility. The commitments of time and capital make this inevitable.

Fourth: complex technologies demand the skills of a wide range of occupations. Men with the requisite skills must be found and continually kept active. This takes planning so that the specialist is not alternately over and under utilized. This seems to be happening in the space program. The huge push to put a man on the moon necessitated the employment of thousands of technicians who became well-integrated research teams. With the reduction in spending for space programs after 1967, many of these teams have been disbanded and scattered. If, in years to come, new monies are pumped into the space effort, teams will have to be constituted at great expense, wasting time and effort.

A fifth imperative of complex cybernetic technologies is a need for a new *form* of organization to supplement that of hierarchical bureaucracy. A single word to characterize this new form of organization has not emerged but it involves "committees," "work teams," "task forces," and the like. In these efforts, decisions are reached not by a single authoritative individual, but by groups composed of men with differing specialized talents whose pooled knowledge surpasses that of any individual. Galbraith (1967:60–66) has pointed out that in this context the nominal head of a unit is extremely reluctant to countermand the "advice" of such experts. Certainly the technical expertise which subordinates now often command compromises the authoritarian bureaucratic structure. Colonels in World War II who had been raised in the tradition of the bureaucratic army often found to their dismay that they had to rely on the judgments of corporals who had been trained to "read" radar (Brezinski 1967).

As Galbraith (1967:16–17) says in summary of these five points: "The more sophisticated the technology, the greater, in general, will be all the foregoing requirements. . . . From the time and capital that must be committed, the inflexibility of this commitment and the needs of large organizations...comes the necessity for planning." As we shall see, the necessity of planning injects a host of new problems into the crucible of industry.

The Human Meanings of Automation

Automation changes our view of the world in at least two different but complementary ways. It makes us think small and bigger at the same time. So that a computer system will operate, all relevant factors must be defined and *objectified* to a greater degree than ever before. This continues the long-term trend discussed earlier in the chapter toward increasing *rationality*. No traditional worker or management technique can remain immune. Unexamined values as diverse as patriotism and romantic love are now more likely to be analyzed and dissected. This increasing objectification can lead to more awareness and candor in human interaction generally. It can also lead to an overemphasis on those criteria of evaluation that can be quantified and readily monitored. Students can see this problem in the college experience. The goal of liberal arts education is to help make the student a complete and mature person. As objectified and programmed by a computer a liberal arts education becomes an affirmative answer to such questions as: completed English 1A and B; two natural sciences, one with laboratory credit; two years of gym; paid all library fines, and the like.

The new higher degree of objectification leads to new ethical problems both great and mundane (Burke 1966; Dechert 1968). Many illustrations might be drawn from the area of medicine. It goes without saying, for example, that only *pure* water should be used when solutions are being injected into the human blood stream. Pure water has long been packaged in glass ampules, but with the powerful microscopes now available it is possible to detect minute splinters of glass created during the manufacture of the ampules. Thus, the "safe" level of glass slivers in the human blood stream now becomes a question which must be answered by engineers and doctors. Similar questions of how to make products safe are faced daily, or should be faced, in the drug, auto, and food-packaging industries among others.

While cybernation enforces candid attention to detail, it also suggests a new view of the world (Wiener 1966; Peterson 1970a); in the cybernetic framework, actions are seen as parts of a totality rather than as a linear sequence. Within such a view, our standard notions of cause and effect are augmented and modified by a view of interacting processes.

The implications of this change in the machine augmented capacity for thinking are beyond the scope of the present discussion (McLuhan 1962), but their meaning for industrial planning is clear. While the textile manufacturer of 1820 knew that wage rates, taxes, tariffs, machine productivity, market demand and the like determined his profits, he did not have the means of measuring and analyzing their interrelated effects. His contemporary counterpart, however, does have much of the detailed information and data manipulation technology needed to *plan* the best future actions by plotting the mutual interactions of the relevant variables. These requisites for intelligent planning are increasingly available to society at large. Since ancient times visionaries have played with the idea of a perfect society. For the first time we have the material resources and technology to begin the construction of a humane society.

Chapter 4

ORGANIZATIONS IN THE CRUCIBLE

An historical perspective has been used to organize the material of Chapters 2 and 3. Changes in technology were traced from early factory production to automation. This and succeeding chapters focus on the present, selecting specific topics to illustrate a range of social problems manifest in the crucible of industry. Here we focus on social technology, examining some of the many forms of organization which have evolved in the wide range of contemporary industrial settings.

Whenever a number of people are required to perform a task, problems of coordination come to the fore, and the success of the venture is often determined by how well these problems are resolved. But the problems of coordination do not stay solved, for the organizational forms which have been created, such as bureaucracy discussed in the last chapter, tend to take on a defensive life of their own. Thus, they may create as many problems as they solve. This chapter focuses on four areas of organizational dynamics which are vitally important in the industrial order.

The first part of the chapter examines the evolving role differentiation within industrial organizations and identifies the sorts of social problems created in the process. The second part focuses on the recent emergence of a particular form of large organization, the conglomerate corporation, examines the reasons for its emergence, and outlines its ideological rationale. The third part focuses on a number of organizational forms which are replacing the reliance on bureaucracy and tries to show the conditions favoring each. The final section examines labor unions, a type of organization in the immediate environment of industrial firms which has long tried to modify industry's actions. The emergence and pathology of unions, as well as current union organizational efforts among California agricultural workers are studied in order to understand why labor unions have developed and survived in the crucible of industry.

Social Technology Today

Work activities have been coordinated in diverse ways in preindustrial societies. Age, sex, race, caste, community, and family were important and are still relevant today. But since the Industrial Revolution, the focus has continually shifted from these tradition-bound statuses. This first part of Chapter 4 traces the changing social technology of industrial work in order to focus more clearly on some of the tensions in the contemporary scene which will be discussed in later sections of the chapter.

CHANGING PATTERNS OF INDUSTRIAL ORGANIZATION

The following enumeration of work roles shows the changing patterns of industrial organization since the advent of the Industrial Revolution 200 years ago. In the machine-tending technologies discussed in Chapter 2, there was an *owner-entrepreneur,* a few *foremen* who gave orders in the owner's name, and a number of *workers* who tended large single purpose machines. In craftfactory technologies of the same era, the *owner* related directly to master *craftsmen* and *apprentices* who were bound together in *craftguild unions.* In both these systems the number of persons in a company rarely exceeded 200, and the owner was in a position to know, as well as be known, by all his "hands."

Mass Production. With the introduction of the assembly line and related technologies in the era of mass production discussed in Chapter 3, the coordination of many more sorts of personnel became imperative; bureaucracy made this possible. The *owner* withdrew from the day-to-day operations and these activities were increasingly taken over, in what has widely been seen as a "managerial revolution," by a cadre of salaried *managers* (Berle and Means 1932). Their decisions were transmitted to the *blue-collar machine operatives* by a small army of *white-collar functionaries.* The line between manager and white-collar functionary was not always easy to draw at first, but it became clearer, for increasingly the functionaries performed routine tasks and had no chance of moving into managerial ranks with decision-making power and prestige (Mills 1951). While the older forms of organization had focused almost entirely on production, the bureaucratic "line" organization of mass production was augmented by a number of kinds of *staff specialists* who brought technical knowledge to bear on specific nonproduction problems such as sales, engineering, finance, research, and industrial unions. Such an organization could coordinate the efforts of tens of thousands of corporation employees.

With the advent of mass production came the development of a new sort of workmen's association, composed not of workers in a single occupation but of all workers in the same factory irrespective of job. Manufacturers were originally very hostile to *industrial* labor unions, such as the United Auto Workers and the Steel Workers of America, because they were seen as a threat to managerial control and worker loyalty. Management and union interests have made an accommodation to each other with the aid of the federal government working through the National Labor Relations Board over the past thirty-five years. While labor and management still use the rhetoric of conflict, most CIO (Congress of Industrial Organizations) unions can be considered, from an organizational point of view, as an integral part of the corporation's labor relations department (Van de Vall 1970; Peterson 1970b). We will discuss this point further below.

Automation. The era of automation has further altered the form of industrial organization. Ownership which earlier had been vested in an individual or family diffuses to a great number of stockholders, so that ownership is more nearly divorced from managerial control (Hacker 1965). The American Telephone and Telegraph Corporation, for example, now has over one million stockholders. The only power any but the few largest of these "owners" has is to sell or buy more stock. It is ironic to note that while factory organization originally consisted of owner and worker, with complete automation the owner will be replaced by salaried managers and the worker will be replaced by machines! The industrial organization is increasingly made up of elements *between* owner and worker which have come into prominence only in this century.

At the top are *managers.* Below this level the earlier distinction between line and staff has become very nearly meaningless. This is because technology is so sophisticated production personnel must have staff skills, and staff jobs are more intimately involved with the daily problems of production (Perrow 1970; Goldner 1970). In mass production, the staff *advised* production personnel; in automation, authority is not nearly so centralized in one position, and each kind of expert cooperates and competes with others for power and prestige. Taken together these various experts are identified by John Kenneth Galbraith (1967) as comprising the *techno-structure.* Below this level are diverse technicians and workers. As mentioned in the last chapter, the distinction between blue- and white-collar work becomes academic in automated conditions. The term used in talking about automated machine monitors and repairmen who oversee production and clerical tasks is *technicians.*

As organizations move toward fully automated machine technologies, the *industrial* union, founded on the principle that all workers in a factory should be organized into the same union local, is dissolving. It is being replaced by a number of worker organizations resembling the old *craft* unions in that they bring together persons of the same skill irrespective of place of employment. These neocraft unions are usually organized as professional associations (Foote 1953). While corporations once had only to negotiate with one union, they will now increasingly have to deal with many associations which represent one or another technical speciality. We will focus on these new employee associations below.

MONOPOLY TO CONGLOMERATES AND ENTREPRENEURS AGAIN

The truly automated concern may employ many fewer workers in a given *plant* than is characteristic in mass production technologies where mile-long factories employ 20,000 workers under one roof. Many more workers, however, may be employed by one firm than ever before because of the rapid rate of corporate "conglomeration." Like the older process of monopoly building, conglomeration involves the absorption of many companies by a few, but the form this process takes is new. The intent of monopoly or trust building was to gain sufficient domination in a particular product or market area to set prices without regard to competition. This crass form of monopolization reached its pinnacle in the railroad, petroleum, tobacco, banking, and steel industries about the turn of the century, and the "level of concentration"—the proportion of an industry controlled by a few large concerns—has not increased appreciably in most basic industries over the ensuing half-century (Bain 1959:187–207; Cochran 1957).

While increasing monopolization is a thing of the past in most industries, a new form of giant organization has emerged in the last decade; it is called the *conglomerate*. These corporations result from the diversification from one product market into many unrelated products. For the most part, conglomeration is the product not of internal growth of corporations, but of the acquisition of one corporation by another. Textron Corporation, one of the early leaders in this movement, exemplifies the process of conglomeration (Child 1969:28–32). In 1949 it was a fully integrated medium-sized firm in the stable low profit and low growth textile industry. In that year it began to sell some of its least profitable facilities and buy companies with high growth potential in widely scattered industries. Through mergers it has become, by 1972, one of America's 100 largest corporations with significant manufacturing facilities in thirteen different industries.

This process of conglomeration has become important only since World War II, but by the late 1960s, according to the *Wall Street Journal*, it had become a "mania." In 1965, 83 percent of all corporate mergers were of the conglomerate type, by 1968 this figure had reached 90 percent, and the business of corporate conglomeration became so brisk that a special magazine began publication to keep up with the avalanche (*Wall Street Journal* February 10, 1969:1). The process and pathology of conglomeration will be treated in a later part of this chapter. While the trend has been toward organizational bigness and complexity, a counter trend is also noteworthy. New forms of small businesses have emerged, particularly in service industries. The ways in which the owner of a retail automobile dealership or Colonel Sanders Fried Chicken franchise are different from the entrepreneur of old will be explored in a later part of this chapter.

Conglomerate Organization

The number of conglomerate corporations has increased rapidly since 1960, and the leading conglomerates have become huge. Most of this growth has come not by the internal expansion of companies but through the acquisition of other firms. In this section we will look at some of the "growing pains" associated with this process, paying particular attention to the reasons, both economic and ideological, for their growth, and the role of the federal government in the process.

SYNERGISTICS: THE IDEOLOGY OF CONGLOMERATION

This term "synergy" is derived from the Greek *synergos,* meaning "cooperation," and was given its modern meaning by an early American sociologist, Lester F. Ward (1907:171–84). It has been adopted by conglomerate executives as an ideological defense of the benefits of conglomerate organization over classical single industry corporations. For example, Sperry Rand Corporation produces a wide range of different products and justifies this by saying it can be more productive in each of these areas because it is involved in each of the others. This is synergistic.

Synergistics may make for savings where technical, managerial, or marketing facilities and techniques can be shared. As a case in point, the Singer Sewing Machine Company has branched out into the manufacture of other household appliances which it can sell through its hundreds of retail outlets created as home sewing centers. Synergistics can work for those on the other side of the law as well. The same set of bootleggers and local political officials who operate the venerable and well organized traffic in illegal "moonshine" whiskey in the southeastern United States apparently now handle the distribution of counterfeit money and stolen automobiles *Nashville Tennessean* October 13, 1967:3). The parallel diversification of the Mafia from illegal alcohol trafficking after the repeal of prohibition into other rackets, all of which involve the provision of an illegal service to a willing client, provides an excellent example of synergistics in practice (Cressey 1969:72–108; *Time* August 22, 1969).

Over the past decade the management of Litton Industries has had outstanding success in building a small concern into a conglomerate giant. This success is a result of bringing modern managerial skills to companies which are financially sound but managerially backward. While managerial reorganization and other synergistic strategies may be effective in some cases, the long-term low profitability of most conglomerates suggests that synergistics is no organizational panacea (Collins and Preston 1968). The situations in which the term has been invoked suggests that synergistics is an ideological weapon used in the defense of conglomerate mergers against the suspicions of dubious investors and government critics (Manne 1965).

THE QUEST FOR STOCK MARKET "PERFORMANCE"

Many conglomerate mergers combine a corporation which is rich in liquid capital, such as an insurance firm, with one which is short on capital for expansion but has a special asset such as technical expertise, patents, contracts, or the like. The newly formed combine can show stockholders of the first company an exciting growth potential and can show stockholders of the second the capital necessary for rapid expansion. In some instances, the benefits of conglomeration are real, and stock investors follow the prospects of mergers quite closely.

As a result, merger rumors usually send stock prices higher. In just one day, for example, the stock of Metromedia went up 15 percent when merger with Transamerica Corporation was rumored (*Wall Street Journal* October 11, 1968:3). As one might expect, this has tempted corporation officials to generate rumors while they bought or sold stock. Such dealing must be done through associates to avoid the detection of stock manipulation. For several large and well-known corporations the purchase and selling of stock amid merger rumors has become a major source of profit (Stabler 1969). For example, Loew's theaters recently made a gross profit of 28.5 million dollars trading in the stock of the Commercial Credit Corporation. In another venture, Loew's bought a large block of B. F. Goodrich stock at $41.00 a share and was soon offered $77.00 a share for them (Berton 1969). Such practices though not always strictly illegal still add a dangerous volatility to the stock market.

Dirty Pooling. A wide range of accounting practices has been employed to exaggerate the performance of conglomerate corporations, and these practices seem to have no other intent than to deceive (*Wall Street Journal* July 25, 1968:1). One case may serve as an example. A conglomerate "wonder" called Automatic Sprinkler reported earnings of $9,200,000 in 1967, a jump of more than 110 percent over 1966 earnings. The price of the stock jumped as a result of this "performance." However, the combined 1966 earnings of Automatic Sprinkler and the companies it had absorbed in 1967 were over $10,800,000! As the *Wall Street Journal* commented, it would be more realistic to say the company *lost* nearly two million dollars than to say it more than doubled its earnings (Stabler 1968: 12). *Barron's Weekly,* a business publication, characterizes this and other related auditing practices which involve the pooling of assets for corporation reports as "dirty pooling" (July 15, 1968:1). The association of professional accountants has worked out procedures for its members in an effort to forestall dirty pooling, but new tactics of financial manipulation emerge as soon as old ones are discredited (*Wall•Street Journal* March 17, 1971:6).

The success of the performance idea depends on the image of corporation management, its product, and the corporation itself. Thus, a company which trades primarily in fried chicken franchises has recently given itself the grand title "Performance Systems Corporation." Older companies even change their names to fit a new and desired image. For example, General Shoe has become Genesco and United Tire and Rubber Company has become Uniroyal. Such face lifting is not cheap: City Service Petroleum Company spent at least $20 million to become Citgo (Weil 1968:18).

In all this, the symbols of automation, cybernetics, synergistics, and the like are being used to cover age-old practices of financial manipulation. One may argue that the stock market is a gambling game and that there should be little social concern for its losers. But a stock market panic, born of merger mania, is a very real possibility in spite of all the regulatory mechanisms which have been developed since the great crash of 1929. Such a market disaster would be a most serious social problem, resulting in the loss of jobs, savings, insurance premiums, and pension rights for millions of citizens who have never dabbled in the stock market.

GOVERNMENT ACTION AND THE GENERAL GOOD

The federal government has been firmly committed to protecting the competitive market economy since the beginning of the century. It has moved to dismantle price-fixing monopolies and continues to do so. Several years ago, for example, General Electric, Westinghouse, and several other companies were convicted of conspiring to fix the prices of heavy electrical equipment. More recently Rexall Drugs, Bristol-Myers, and thirteen other drug companies have been indicted for conspiracy to fix the world price of quinine (*Wall Street Journal* Oct. 28, 1968:1).

At the same time, the government has acted to *maintain* an appearance of competition in oligopolistic industries by buying items at special prices from the smaller companies in the industry. For example, the federal government has, since 1967, helped to maintain the solvency of the American Motors Company, joining both General Motors and Ford in this effort (Proxmire 1966; Pearlstine 1971:4). For all its efforts, the government has not been able to reverse the tide of industry concentration. It has been nearly powerless to stem the growth of conglomerates because antitrust laws were formulated to prevent one corporation from gaining control of a single industry rather than preventing its strategic location in several (Dirlam and Kahn 1954; Kaysen and Turner 1959; Kohlmeier 1969:28, 1970:4). Yet it probably does not make sense to break up these large combines. In the long run, the support of weak companies such as American Motors makes no more sense than the current price support system in agriculture, which was intended to save the small family farm but has had the consequence of accelerating the trend toward large-scale corporate farming (Goldschmidt 1947; *Barron's Weekly* August 5, 1968:3; London and Anderson 1970).

In practice, federal tax policy has unintentionally fostered a special but widely practiced merger gambit which is sometimes referred to by insiders as "plunder and run." In such cases a firm is acquired because it has a single asset strongly desired by the absorbing company. The asset may be patents to an important invention, liquid capital, a well organized research staff, a respected brand name, or any one of a number of elements which may be attractive to the purchasing company. Taking that asset, the absorbing company then sells or closes down the manufacturing operations of the absorbed company. This absorbing company can afford to treat the other in such a way because it can write-off any losses incurred to reduce its own federal taxes. Should the government, in effect, subsidize such merger tactics? Clearly they affect the jobs of many and may disrupt the prosperity of entire communities or may create new employment opportunities. In this case, as in those already discussed, what is needed is a means to follow and evaluate the various gains and losses caused by conglomerate mergers. We will return to this perplexing problem in Chapter 6.

Organizational Decentralization

While industrial firms have become ever larger and managerial decision making has been increasingly centralized, a counter trend has also gained importance in recent decades. In this age of giant corporations, 1500 businesses are incorporated each working day of the year (*Wall Street Journal* February 12, 1968:1)! Some of these are independent small businesses not organizationally unlike those of 200 years ago, but most, like the locally owned franchised outlet for a fast-food chain, are affiliated in one way or another with larger firms. What is more, some departments in large firms operate in large part as if they were independent organizations (Thompson 1967; Perrow 1970).

These diverse organizational forms represent attempts to deal with problems resulting from changes in machine technology and the environments of the organization which cannot adequately be solved by conventional bureaucratic mechanisms. Several frequently occurring types of decentralized organizational forms and the context in which they emerge are explored in this part of the chapter.

THE ORGANIZATION PROFESSIONAL

Bureaucracy is the best form of social technology for processing standardized and simple routines in large organizations as noted in Chapter 3. When tasks are more complex and technical, bureaucratic forms do not work well and persons trained in a special area of knowledge are required. If such problems arise only occasionally, as when an architectural firm is asked to design a new factory or an accounting firm is asked to audit financial records, such expert services may be contracted out to specialized firms which exclusively provide such services (Chandler 1964).

When, however, complex problems occur often and persons with specialized knowledge are required on a more regular basis, firms often employ experts and place them in special departments within the firm. Examples include engineering, marketing, research, industrial relations, and legal departments. The persons working in each of these are trained to see the world and the problems faced by the firm from a special perspective, and thus they often come in conflict with the interest of the larger organization which is oriented to profit making through production (Goldner 1970; Perrow 1970).

Scientists in Industry. Of the various competing interests, the conflict between the organization and its scientists has been most thoroughly explored (Glaser 1964; Kornhauser 1962; Abrahamson 1967; Ritti 1971). Firms hire scientists and provide them equipment in the expectation that they will make discoveries and perfect products that will enhance future profitability. Thus, the focus is usually on research problems which are, from a scientific perspective, quite mundane. For example, chemists of a soap company may be asked to find a cheap nontoxic foaming agent to add to detergents because customers expect soap to make suds and believe that nonsudsing detergents do not work (Graham 1970).

Scientists, on the other hand, are trained to seek out research problems that are most relevant to generating and testing theory, and they seek to publish the results of their work. From the corporation's perspective, this means scientists want to study esoteric problems and then give away information produced at the firm's expense. While many professionals are willing to work at tasks set by management, they still enjoy a degree of bargaining power with the firm not shared by most other workers. Due to specialized knowledge, professional education, with a power often backed by state law to certify the professional, and recognition of a special status by society, these occupations can restrict their own number and gain salaries higher than they might otherwise command (Hall 1969:70–130). Professional associations which operate much like traditional craft labor unions have been vital in maintaining professional autonomy.

Seeing the power, prestige, and income of professionals, many occupations employed within large organizations have begun to "professionalize" by emulating superficial characteristics of established professions. This trend has become so widespread that Wilensky (1964a) exclaims, "the professionalization of everyone?" As he and others (Etzioni 1969; Glaser 1968; Abrahamson 1967) note, it is much more likely that these occupations will become semiprofessional and have some of the superficial trappings of professionalization including professional associations and codes of ethics without gaining the substance of professional control over recruitment, training, and practice of their own members. In the case of engineers (Goldner and Ritti 1967; Ritti 1971) and librarians (Goode 1961), professionalization has been fostered by the employing organization in order to *restrict* the employee's job freedoms. Put in its simplest form, the managerial strategy can be stated as follows: "You say you are professional. All right, professionals are devoted to service; they do not bargain for wages or compete in a market economy, so be professional by being loyal, hard working, and obedient to the organization."

Guilds versus Change. Seen in a broader perspective, the degree of professionalization of occupations within organizations seems to be the product of several contradictory forces. On the one hand, organizations seeking stability and control bureaucratize jobs as much as possible; on the other hand, occupational groups trying to establish and protect their exclusive right to do certain types of work professionalize jobs as much as possible (Vollmer and Mills 1962; Hall 1968; Montagna 1968). If these two forces alone were in operation, a rigid bureaucratically bounded occupational structure would develop, a structure reminiscent in many ways of the craft guild system of the Middle Ages (Pirenne 1956:75–152; Thrupp 1948:53–102; Zald 1971).

This has not happened in the modern era largely because changes in technology and market demands occur quite rapidly, disrupting the emerging static structure of professional occupations in organizations. The changing fortunes of "ceramic engineering" provide an excellent case in point. For centuries, ceramics were made by craftsmen potters. Then in the early part of this century, with the rapidly expanding use of electricity, ceramic insulators became widely used and the art was consolidated into a separate discipline called ceramic engineering in a number of engineering schools. In the span of just one generation of engineers, however, this ceramic engineering became obsolete with the introduction of plastic insulators. In recent years ceramic engineering again has received a new lease on life, as ceramics are used in various aspects of atomic energy production and in the heat shields of vehicles returning from outer space.

ENTREPRENEURSHIP IN ORGANIZATIONS

The environments of an organization may be unchanging, changing in ways that can be evaluated and predicted by technical experts as just illustrated, or changing in ways unseen by analysis and immune to prediction. Emery and Trist (1965) label this latter environment as *turbulent,* and Perrow (1967:196) notes that such an environment creates special problems for organizational personnel: there must be many "exceptions to organizational routine, no established procedure for seeking solutions, no 'formal' search is undertaken, but instead, one draws upon the residue of unanalyzed experience, on intuition, or relies on chance and guesswork." Under such turbulent conditions, bureaucratic, professional, and craft leadership styles are inappropriate and the organization must rely on what Thompson and Tuden (1959) term "inspirational strategy." This leadership style is here identified as *entrepreneurship.*

The analysis of entrepreneurship in organizations is based on a study (Peterson and Berger 1971) of the popular recorded music industry which has a marketing environment very near the turbulent extreme, depending as it does on the rapidly changing style preferences of millions of predominantly young buyers (McPhee 1966).

The Entrepreneurial Function. The term entrepreneurship when used in contemporary studies of organization usually designates the persons who own a firm (Davis 1968) or the ownership function more abstractly (Becker and Gordon 1966). Used here is Schumpeter's (1934:74–94) more dynamic definition of this leadership style, in which entrepreneurship is seen as a novel combination of the available means of production. Schumpeter stresses that no occupational position or organizational office can be defined as entrepreneurial, although it is often convenient to talk of an entrepreneur. Rather an individual is an entrepreneur only when he actually carries out new combinations. In contrast to the use of the term by Marshall (1925), Parsons and Smelser (1956), and Bain (1959), who identify it with managements, Schumpeter identifies it as a function which may be carried out by persons in many different positions. Schumpeter stresses that such new combinations most often are made by employees of large firms rather than by self-employed businessmen. As described by Schumpeter (1934), the exercise of entrepreneurship requires a mental freedom to work outside normal channels; thus, there is tension between the intermittent organizational need for entrepreneurship and the entrepreneur's empire-building way of working, so that the entrepreneur is likely to find the organization stultifying, while the organization may often find the entrepreneur disruptive.

At least three adaptations to the potential entrepreneur-organization tension are possible. (1) The organization may be small and loosely structured enough that the entrepreneur can manage his own business. This is exemplified by the classical entrepreneur of the early stages of the Industrial Revolution, and in the recording industry by the independent record producers who emerged in the mid 1960s when the market was extremely turbulent. (2) The organization, alone or more commonly in conjunction with other organizations, may render the environment nonturbulent, thus nearly eliminating the need for entrepreneurship as exemplified by the Tin Pan Alley era of the recording business from 1925 until about 1955 when the five leading companies enjoyed an oligopolistic control of the market (Peterson and Berger 1972). (3) Large organizations may adapt to the requirements of entrepreneurship, which occurs when the organization cannot reduce the turbulence of at least one important segment of its environment. This adaptation took place in the popular music industry when conditions of moderately great turbulence characterized the organization's market environment between 1955 and 1965.

Organizational Adaptation to Turbulence. The organizational adaptations to greater and lesser turbulence (adaptations 1 and 2) are discussed below. First the record industry's adaptation to entrepreneurship with moderately high turbulence is discussed. Such adaptation involves three organizational strategies. (1) The segment of the organization which interacts with the turbulent element of the environment is segregated from other segments as completely as possible. (2) Within this environmentally linked segment, entrepreneurship is isolated into a specific role which is linked with a number of specialists. (3) The financial risks of each entrepreneurial decision is minimized.

The integrated recording company is typically an element of a conglomerate involved in most of the following activities: television networks, music publishing houses, music instrument companies, direct sales organizations, talent-booking agencies, and movie studios (*Business Week*, 1967).

The recording company division of the conglomerate is usually divided into three divisions, one of which is the manufacturing division. Inputs include master stamping plates and record jackets. Records are manufactured and packaged on highly standardized machinery so that no matter what sorts of sounds are recorded, be they Gregorian chants or electronic rock, the stamping and packaging routines are unaffected. Stamping machinery can be reset to manufacture one or another record within a matter of minutes to accommodate market demands, and any excess demand can be subcontracted to independent stamping plants. Thus, the manufacturing division of the company is fully segregated from environmental turbulence, and as might be expected, this division is quite bureaucratic in organization.

Sales and promotion comprise the second division. It is organized on a territorial basis, and like most sales divisions a large part of its organizational activities are focused on the undertakings of its own agents. The division has a flat organizational chart, depending on frequent telephone contacts, internal publications, and money incentive plans to coordinate and motivate its far-flung agents (Shemel and Krasilovsky 1965; Hirsch 1969). The segregation of the sales and promotion division from environmental turbulence is not complete, as the wrong promotional drive may "kill" a potential hit record; for the most part, the department operates as if it were unaffected by turbulent aspects of the environment.

The third division of the record company is production, which is organizationally segregated from the other two main divisions of the corporation. It is expected to create a succession of hit records and is thus more directly in contact with the turbulent environment. The division is typically headed by a corporation vice-president, but his task is primarily to maintain a semblance of financial order over the activities of different types of professionals, craftsmen, and artists. Many of these work on a job-contract basis, often rent recording studios, so personnel and equipment resources are retained only so long as they are needed. The production division is loosely organized to adapt to continuous change in the turbulent market, much as in the construction industry as described by Stinchcombe (1959).

Within the turbulent environment-oriented division of the organization, the entrepreneurial function is isolated, as far as possible into a specific role. Focusing entrepreneurship in one role not only facilitates the organization's adaptation to environmental turbulence, but also simplifies organizational control over this amethodical function. In the record industry this is the producer, still called an artist and repertoire man or A and R man.

In creating a record, the recording company producer interacts with numerous kinds of technical specialists who make a specific contribution to the final product. In contrast to these specialists, the producer must be a generalist: as one respondent noted the producer is "The guy who puts it all together, the guy that can hear what will sell." Thus, in the recording industry the entrepreneurial function of making novel combinations of available resources to achieve success in a turbulent market is isolated from other technical roles.

At least four different tactics have been developed in the recording industry to limit the liability of entrepreneurship. In some particulars the tactics are unique to this industry, but many similar strategies can be found in other industries.

First, the discretion of each entrepreneur is limited. While corporation executives say they give their producers a free hand with money to create hits, they retain considerable control: for example, although the producer signs new talent, a corporation vice-president must countersign the contract, and the vice-president also must approve the budget estimate for each recording project. How much discretion the company producer is given in practice depends on the sales of his prior productions. Parallel criteria seem to operate for extending discretion to editors in book publishing houses, and in granting basic research funds to scientists.

The second organizational strategy to reduce entrepreneurial liability is by increasing as much as possible the number of entrepreneurial decisions while minimizing the investment in each. Because there is no rational way of knowing which recordings will be successful in a turbulent market, the recording company employs a number of producers, each of whom produces records for half a dozen or more artists. In this way, the number of entrepreneurial decisions is quite large. At Columbia Records, for example, an average of one new album is released each day, and ten new single 45 r.p.m. records are released a week (*Business Week*, 1967). Most master tapes in the popular music field are produced for less than $5,000, and the total cost of production, manufacturing, and promotion is often under $50,000. Columbia has annual sales in excess of $200 million so its investment in each record is not great. It is rational to release a wide range of songs in the hope of producing a hit.

Third, the risks of entrepreneurship may be decreased by developing a means of rapidly monitoring the market success of each entrepreneurial decision and thus each entrepreneur. This is easily accomplished in the record industry, for the market life of a single 45 r.p.m. record is usually only 60 days and is rarely over 120 days; the market life of long-playing records can be accurately estimated in the same length of time (Hirsch 1969). Record sales performance is even more rapidly projected by *Billboard* and *Cashbox* magazine listings of current hits. Their charts are based largely on jukebox and radio-air play which tend to lead sales performance by several weeks; thus, whether a producer is currently in touch with his potential audience or not can be known within a matter of weeks. This knowledge aids company executives in deciding whether to heavily promote, to release without fanfare, or not to release records similar to recent releases.

Finally, entrepreneurial liability is limited by rewarding or firing entrepreneurs on the basis of success in the turbulent environment. The producer is hired on his presumed ability to find and produce that elusive novelty sound which will generate hit records. As one producer commented, "They keep me because I hear commercial, I like commercial...my ear is like a public ear." Like recording artists, the new producer is given a short-term contract while the company retains a first option to renew his contract; in this way the company can keep the successful producer from going to a rival company while quickly getting rid of those who lose the magic touch.

Adaptation to Variations in Turbulence. The environment with which the producer deals is not always equally turbulent, for the degree of turbulence in the popular music field has dramatically changed since World War II. Periods of both greater and lesser turbulence than that assumed in the discussion above provide the opportunity to examine the correlation between changes in turbulence, entrepreneurship, and organizational structure; if organizational forms which allow for entrepreneurship are adaptations to a turbulent environment, then variations in the degree of turbulence should cause variations in the scope of entreprenurship.

LESSER TURBULENCE   Until about 1955 the four largest recording companies maintained an oligopolistic control of the popular music market (Peterson and Berger 1972). They were, in effect, able to manage the rate of innovation in musical styles and could realize a safe, if not spectacular, return on almost all recordings made. This ability to reduce market turbulence shaped producers' roles. A relatively few songs were recorded and the only market question was whether the potential audience wanted to hear it rendered by Bing Crosby, Frank Sinatra, Vaughn Monroe, Doris Day, or Nat King Cole. The corporations focused on building and maintaining stars and were quite successful in monopolizing radio-air play by bribing disc jockeys and other radio industry personnel. These bribes came to be known as "payola." A Detroit promoter said, "In those days you paid your money and got your hit. Today, nobody can predict what will get played on the air" (Hirsch 1969:47).

Given such stable market conditions a system developed in which entrepreneurial discretion was slight; talent was chosen by corporation executives and assigned to producers. A master producer kept whatever star performer he wanted and assigned new artists to one of several journeyman producers under his supervision. The best known of the master producers was Mitch Miller. Producers in the jazz and classical music fields which have relatively stable and predictable markets were not allowed to exercise much entrepreneurial discretion. In these contexts, the producer was a salaried employee and was considered one craftsman among others. Thus low environmental turbulence was associated with a formalized organizational structure and slight entrepreneurship.

GREATER TURBULENCE   Since the early 1950s, a number of interrelated technological, market, and organizational changes as well as the rock music revolution (Belz 1969; Carey 1969; Denisoff and Peterson 1972; Luthe 1968) have taken place which have made the popular recording industry's environment much more turbulent than it had been (Peterson and Berger 1972). As the market became less controlled, the master producer system gave way to the system described above in which a number of company producers, each working without direct supervision, competed in the pursuit of the novel sound.

In recent years, this organizational adaptation has proven too cumbersome for the exigencies of a hyperturbulent market; for even if the producer could hear the sound that would sell one year, he often proved deaf the next. Thus he became a liability to the corporation. A host of independent producers, unfettered by organizational complexities, formed their own companies and in a very few years ended the dominance of the large established corporations in the popular music market (Hirsch 1969; Peterson and Berger 1972). The most notable of these independents, Phil Spector, was well on his way to making his first million dollars while still in his teens.

Faced with this new source of competition, the large corporations have employed at least four strategies to regain their preeminence in the volatile popular music market. First, they buy master tapes from the freelance, independent producers, taking a profit on promotion, manufacturing, and distribution. Second, they have purchased a number of the most successful independents and absorbed them into the corporate organization (Wenner 1969). Third, a strategy between these two has developed: the corporation gives an independent producer his own department within the larger corporation.

Finally, the company may retreat from the most turbulent segment of the environment. RCA Victor, one of the largest firms in the industry, has adopted this strategy, having gotten out of the rock and soul music markets, while concentrating on the less turbulent country, easy listening, and classical fields. As one would expect from the hypothesis concerning the relationship between turbulence and organization structure, RCA Victor adheres more closely than any other company to the master producer system characteristic of the earlier era.

A general reduction in market turbulence may also be taking place, for in recent years the established corporations in the industry have also been engaged in an aggressive campaign of mergers (*Business Week* 1970). They have sought not only to absorb independent producers but also to control the media through which music is introduced to the audience. If this re-enoligopolization is successful, it is predicted that there will be a return to something structurally equivalent to the master producer system which involves a great reduction in the entrepreneurial scope of the producer's role.

Entrepreneurship Reconsidered. Like other venerable concepts in social science, the term entrepreneurship has often been used as a descriptive label for a specific phenomenon embedded in a single historical context. However Schumpeter's definition of the term entrepreneurship (1934) as a novel recombination of preexisting elements implies that entrepreneurship is a process variable which may be seen in the leadership roles of widely divergent historical and organizational contexts.

Using his definition, the conditions in which entrepreneurship will emerge and the organizational strategies adopted to contain its disruptive effects have been specified by examining entrepreneurship in the popular music industry. This industry is undoubtedly unique in some ways, but turbulent environments probably exist wherever an organization's product must suit fashion or novelty. The fact that the movie industry has gone through strikingly parallel organizational changes in adapting to similar variations in environmental turbulence over the past forty years (Gans 1964; Penn 1969) suggests that these correlated market and organizational changes are not due to unique circumstances in the music industry.

As Hirsh (1969) has noted, roles similar to the popular music producers should exist in the theater, book publishing, clothing industry, stock market, and in politics, where the party system does not successfully pre-structure the choice of candidates. In a somewhat broader sense, many of the same sorts of entrepreneurial exigencies exist for research-oriented organizations. The term academic entrepreneur is appropriately applied to directors of research institutes and to persons in like positions, for they must juggle many factors of production in the turbulent environment of federal, state, foundation, and university funding.

While focusing on entrepreneurship in economic activity, Schumpeter (1934) noted that the art of recombination extends to the moral, cultural, and social organizational spheres as well; thus, the focus of entrepreneurial recombination need not be the economic means of production. Becker (1963) has used the term "moral entrepreneur" to describe the individual whose combination of various value elements form a new ethic. Finally, Mills (1951) has used the term "new entrepreneur" to refer to organizational employees who focus on recombinations of elements within organizations, and the relations between organizations which have become stultified by their own procedural complexities.

Stripped of its nineteenth-century trappings, entrepreneurship seems to be an important component of leadership styles in diverse contemporary organizational contexts which face a turbulent environment.

THE SELF-EMPLOYED EMPLOYEE

Franchised dealerships have expanded rapidly in number and economic importance over recent decades in a wide range of different industries. The *Wall Street Journal* (July 29, 1968:1) estimates that in 1957, 50,000 franchise operations had sales of $2.5 billion, while a decade later eight times as many operators were doing sixteen times as much business. There are franchise operations of many different sorts, ranging from large Holiday Inns and automobile dealerships to neighborhood chicken shacks and Tastee Freeze outlets. All are independently financed operations which sell in an open and often highly competitive market some product or service which is provided to them by a single large corporation. Thus, they are neither totally independent nor simply departments of a firm.

Corporations lose some degree of control by dealing through franchised outlets rather than incorporating the outlets' services directly into the firm, but this arrangement has a number of advantages. First, the franchisee's investment in facilities, machinery, equipment, and inventory make it possible for corporations to expand rapidly without depending on their own capital resources. This use of dealers' money was important in the early days of rapid expansion in the auto and oil industries, and in large part explains the explosive expansion of fast-food corporations in recent years (Rottenberg 1969).

Second, the franchise arrangement shifts the risk of financial loss from the corporation to the dealer (*Wall Street Journal* April 19, 1971:4). For example, dealers may be forced to take articles they do not want in order to get those which are selling well. In this way automobile and shoe companies have been able to pass some of the cost of their own mistakes on to the dealer. In particularly bad years, dealers may be forced to buy many more items than they can sell at the full price in order to keep their dealership, thus absorbing much of the financial loss which would otherwise be felt by corporations.

Such tactics have led gas station franchisees to see themselves in a state of bondage to their parent corporations (Hyatt 1969). An excellent scholarly account of the conflicts between corporations and their dealers is found in Macaulay's (1966) study of new car dealers. Leonard and Weber (1970) argue that the poor workmanship and unnecessary repairs often made by auto dealers result in large part from the narrow profit margins set for them by auto manufacturers. Kramer and Austin (1971), however, have found that repair garages which are not linked to auto manufacturers are no less flagrant in overcharging for car repairs.

Third, franchising may reduce the vulnerability of the corporation in a number of ways. Taxes, government regulations, and code enforcement are usually less stringent on small businesses than on large corporations. The creation of franchise dealerships has helped to frustrate the wholesale unionization of corporation employees. What is more, legal and financial liability as well as consumer complaints are more likely to focus on the local dealer than on the larger corporation.

Fourth, the franchising arrangement is an excellent arrangement for motivating key personnel. Since the dealer is "working for himself" there is no need for close supervision by the corporation, for the dealer himself will pay close attention to details which affect profitability of the outlet he runs. For these reasons, franchise arrangements are likely to be found where worksites are widely scattered and small, where customers must be sought out, where personalized service to customers is important, where spoilage or wastage is an important problem, or where low paid unskilled employees requiring close supervision make up a large part of operating costs.

In the past, franchising operations have grown in new industries (automobile, gasoline retailing) or industries where corporations are replacing independent operators (restaurants, drugstores, motels). They are becoming important in industries where it is impossible for the home office to adequately supervise a far-flung and diverse operation.

SOUL OWNERS

Segregation and discrimination in the United States have provided a continuous opportunity for legitimate and underworld black business to serve the ethnic community. Black-owned barbershops, taverns, grocery stores, funeral parlors, taxi companies, and similar service concerns have thrived for these reasons. While these companies are relatively conspicuous, their economic importance is more apparent than real according to Frazier (1957). For example, in Nashville, Tennessee black-owned businesses today account for only five percent of the total black retail market. In addition, Blacks have long run branches of businesses which provide illegal services in the ghetto. In effect, political machines and racketeers have long been "equal opportunity" employers. But, with the demise of the political machines and the increasing police pursuit of organized crime, these business opportunities are likely to diminish as well.

If the prospects for independent family-run black businesses are dim, the prospects may be better for franchise operations of the sort described in the section above, and a new magazine *Black Enterprise* accents them. The federal government and private foundations (Sutton 1968), as well as large corporations (Haddad and Pugh 1969; Sethi 1970), and cooperative ventures of Blacks themselves (Blundell 1968; Watermulder 1969) have provided money, training, and other services to Blacks attempting to establish businesses. In some cases, the products are ethnic in nature (Carlson 1968), but more often they are goods and services sold in black areas.

While efforts to promote black ownership have been couched in terms of the highest ideals (Ginsberg 1964; Nelson 1969) their success has been spotty. In 1967 before the effort to recruit Blacks had begun, 28,000 new automobile dealers included only one Black; three years later after many more franchises had been given to Blacks only thirty were still in business. The nonsurvivors included such notables as baseball player Ernie Banks (Connor 1970). Of course there is a high attrition rate among all new enterprises, but black franchise operators have been particularly vulnerable to some risks because of the location of their dealerships, the nature of their clientele, and their race.

First, dealers have found it difficult to get the continuing financing needed to build a business in the critical first years (Schorr 1969, 1971b). Second, black dealers have lost sales to Whites because they could not arrange as attractive credit terms for customers (Connor 1970). Third, insurance costs in ghetto areas have more than doubled in recent years (*Wall Street Journal* July 11, 1968:22) as have levels of theft and vandalism. Fourth, some Negro owners have been reluctant to overtly promote campaigns to "buy black" for fear of offending their white sponsors (Sturdivant 1969). Finally, black businessmen have been pressured to make sizeable contributions to various black causes. These range from donations to churches and "taxes" to black militants, to extortion by black gangs who vandalize establishments and harass customers unless they are paid to "protect" the establishment (Laing 1970).

Critics of the franchising policies of automobile, gasoline, grocery, and fast-food companies have suggested that most of the dealerships granted Blacks are ones which Whites had abandoned for the same reasons as those just cited (Connor 1970). A final paradox in the efforts to develop black business is that many potential recruits have been induced to take managerial positions in white corporations. All in all, self-employment may prove to be a small but symbolically important avenue of mobility for Blacks as it has been for blue-collar workers, as we will note in the next chapter.

Unions: Established, Corrupt, and Nascent

In the introduction to this chapter, we noted that for many purposes one might view the well-established industrial union as a part of the corporate organization and that such industrial unions will probably wither away with the advent of full automation. Since automation is mostly a thing of the future, and labor-management relations are by no means always accommodated, unions remain a significant element in the crucible of industry.

Why Unions?

There is no absolute necessity for having industrial labor unions just as there is none for having a stock market. However, as the stock market has served as an important mechanism for amassing capital for industrial expansion, American labor unions have developed to stabilize the cost and supply of labor available for industry. In the process, unions have done much to redress the imbalance in bargaining power between the individual worker and the large corporation. They have helped to prevent corporations from treating blue-collar workers as a commodity that could be bought and sold on a day-by-day basis (Commons 1918). If labor unions had not developed, workers might well have pressed their felt exploitation in the capitalist system in a more political and revolutionary direction (Perlman 1958; Brody 1964). It is significant to note that Karl Marx, the great prophet of the communist revolution, saw labor unions as one of the greatest threats to communist organization of the working classes, because unions would ameliorate rather than eliminate the exploitation of workers.

If employers had treated workers in a thoroughly equitable, paternalistic way, workers probably would not have built labor unions. What is more, it is probably in the long-term interest of a company to give workers the job security, seniority, accident, and retirement benefits which they have won through unionization, because such benefits reduce worker turnover and increase worker loyalty and morale (Van de Vall 1970). But in our competitive industrial system any firm which did unilaterally grant all of these benefits would be priced out of the market. Thus, union organization has forced all companies in an industry to cooperate in their *own* best interests (Grob 1969).

In addressing the question, Why unions? It must be added that the great surge of industrial union organization between 1934 and 1952 would have been impossible without the protection of the federal government. With the coming of the New Deal in the 1930s, the federal government began to foster union organization both through favorable court rulings and the enactment of new legislation such as the National Labor Relations Act of 1935 (Bernstein 1966; Gregory 1961). Of course, every institution takes its being partially from the protection of law, but the legal crutch is more obvious in the emergence of industrial union organizations, as it was in the case of the joint stock corporation which emerged fifty years earlier under the protection of newly enacted corporation law. In both cases, the basic laws were planned and enacted to have specific social and economic effect in the face of specifically felt societal needs (Commons 1951; Coleman 1970).

Several studies have tried to assay, through detailed analyses of wages, whether unions actually have delivered higher wages to their members. These studies show that unionized workers have only slightly higher wages than nonunion members (Rees 1962; Curtin 1965; Lewis 1966). Of course, they cannot show what wage levels would be if there were no unions at all. In practice, nonunion corporations in partially unionized industries are often quite willing to pay their own workers a fraction *over* the union scale to forestall union organization.

Union-won wages are often singled out as a prime cause of price increases and general inflation. For example, one large steel corporation which recently raised its selling price blamed "spiraling labor costs," but according to an economist, if the increased revenue which the price increases will bring were *all* given to the company's hourly workers, it would more than *double* the take home pay of each worker! The argument that unions cause inflation is hard to defend in the light of the fact that prices are rising fastest in fields lacking unions (Malabre 1968).

Technological Change. Technological change has made great new problems for the union. Many of the strongest unions have lost members because of increasing technological unemployment (Stern 1967). Like contemporary corporations, unions have reacted to this change in their environment by forming mergers and diversifying into unrelated labor fields. Thus labor conglomerates are beginning to emerge (Gannon 1968; *Wall Street Journal* May 7, 1968:1). For example, the Laborers International Union, formerly the old Hod Carriers Union, has merged with several other unions employing unskilled labor and now has organized nurses aides, cow hands, dock workers in Samoa, and city employees as members (*Wall Street Journal* July 15, 1968:1, 19). Whether conglomerate unions can speak equally well for all their diverse sorts of members remains to be seen, but available evidence, drawn from the Teamsters Union is not encouraging (James and James 1965:194, 212). Having looked at why labor unions exist, the rest of the chapter examines four organization-based social problems involving contemporary unions, or their leaders.

CURRENT UNION-BUSTING

The managements of many American corporations have an abiding dread of labor unions. They do not want to lose their "managerial prerogatives." Corporation executives focus great amounts of attention, time, and money on curbing union power (Chandler 1964; Goldner 1970), while being relatively complacent about managerial featherbedding and inefficiency. As a case in point, Genesco, a large shoe manufacturer, production consultants have estimated to the horror of management that the leather cutters' inefficient practices cost five million dollars annually, but management is quite unconcerned about another inefficiency located within management which annually costs the corporation ten times as much money.

A classical tactic of chastening worker militance is to threaten employees with the introduction of new labor-saving machines. This tactic was employed 150 years ago in the textile industry and yet again as late as 1968 against craft glass blowers (*Wall Street Journal* March 6, 1968:4). New tactics are employed as well; Texas Instruments, a manufacturer of electronic components, employing primarily women has recently put all of its blue-collar workers on its salary rolls to forestall unionization attempts by the United Auto Workers (*Wall Street Journal* December 1, 1967:1). One age-old tactic, discussed earlier in describing paternalism in textile manufacture, is to move plants from a region with strong unions into a region where unions are weak or unknown. Many companies earlier moved plants to the southeast for this reason (Peterson and Demerath 1965). Now, they move to the Mexican side of the United States-Mexican border, just out of reach of all United States labor laws. In 1958 alone, 66 large plants were moved across the border. The "runaways" include RCA and Motorola corporations attracted by an "inexhaustible labor supply at thirty cents an hour." This tactic is economically feasible because both American and Mexican laws are now written so that import duties need not be paid on goods which are manufactured overseas from components shipped from the United States and then reshipped to the United States as manufactured goods (*Wall Street Journal* February 21, 1969; Holles 1971:1, 14).

In all this, unions and corporations alike act in terms of their own best interests as they understand them at the moment. Regardless of who is "right" in any given case, there seems to be a tremendous waste of human and material resources of the society as a whole. It may be that this waste is a necessary cost for maintaining a free society, but this is at least an empirical question open to review.

CORRUPT UNIONISTS

As noted above, labor unions try to control the supply of labor. A few union leaders have for generations taken the view that they themselves were brokers of labor services and have turned their union positions to personal advantage. A classical means of accomplishing this goal is the "sweetheart" contract in which the employer pays the union leader to agree to lower wages for union members than might be obtained through militant union action. In a related practice, a company may agree to be organized by a "paper local" of one union to avoid genuine unionization. Then again, union leaders may threaten a company with high absenteeism, breakage, or work slow-downs unless a "protection fee" is paid. The air freight industry affords an example of labor racketeering, for in a recent year $2.5 million was pilfered from air freight at Kennedy Airport in New York City. A "consulting firm" formed by Teamster Union officials offered its services to eliminate this theft for any shipper who would pay its fee (*Wall Street Journal* January 5, 1968:1). Here we have a jet age version of the age-old protection racket. As Bell (1959) has noted, such rackets most easily develop where a few workers can effectively disrupt an expensive routine in which time is at a premium. Bell draws his example from the New York docks where, because of the narrow streets, a few men can block the unloading of huge ships which lose thousands of dollars each day they are not underway.

While business-oriented journals and the press generally dwell on *union* corruption, most such corrupt activities require the complicity, if not the active participation, of businessmen or politicians (Tyler 1962).

JAMES R. HOFFA: PRODUCT OF INDUSTRY STRUCTURE

The most colorful labor leader of recent times is James R. Hoffa, past president of the International Brotherhood of Teamsters. He has been the model of the tough, articulate labor organizer; he has also been accused of every crime from jury tampering to consorting with criminals and trucking company owners for his personal gain (James and James 1965). Robert F. Kennedy founded his political career on the pursuit of Hoffa's wrongdoing (Kennedy 1960). That side of Hoffa's career and Kennedy's personal vendetta against him have been reported elsewhere (Zagri 1966; Clay 1965). Without detracting from the man's obvious genius, we want to show that Hoffa, in part, owes his success as a union organizer to the unique structure of the trucking industry (James and James 1965). To do this, it will be helpful to compare trucking with the construction industry and its carpenters union, and here we develop an idea researched by Long (1968b).

Both are large industries employing over a million workers each, and neither is dominated by a small number of large corporations. Unlike most other major contemporary industries, no corporation accounts for even one percent of the business in either industry. Working conditions are alike in the two cases, for workers in trucks and on construction sites work without close supervision. In both, employment varies seasonally, so union job protection helps to stabilize employment. In both industries technological changes are being introduced which threaten worker autonomy and increase worker dependency on union protection. Finally, in both industries strategic work stoppages are expensive to a company and thus effective for the union. Characteristic of strategic work stoppages, Hoffa became a union man the day he led his fellow workers off a loading dock just as a shipment of perishable fruit was being delivered.

There are differences between the two industries as well; a local strike in trucking affects all companies across the nation whose freight is being shipped through the local area. There is no comparable "mushrooming effect" in the construction industry, for work stoppage on a construction site in Memphis has no appreciable effect on construction in Chicago. Trucking companies, by their nature, interlink the nation while construction sites are localized in one city or another. For these reasons, trucking is regulated primarily by federal laws, while construction must conform primarily to local building codes. Finally, trucking firms can, and in the past often did, change their base of operation to avoid strong union locals. Construction corporations obviously do not have this mobility.

Changing Structure. Before World War II both the teamsters and the carpenters unions consisted of loose confederations of strong locals. The carpenters union has retained this locally focused structure while the International Brotherhood of Teamsters has become quite strongly centralized. Hoffa did not begin this centralization process nor did he invent the prime strategy which has made centralization possible, but he has used it to great advantage in his efforts to bring standard rates to all American truck drivers.

In the earlier era, teamster unions were composed almost exclusively of *local* truck drivers of a given city. Drivers on highways between cities were beyond the protection of the union. They drove a prodigious number of hours for low wages; drivers who complained were simply replaced. Hoffa organized these drivers by getting city drivers in a region to stop deliveries to highway shippers until the latter signed a Teamster contract. Once a large area was organized, it was possible to extend the organization by freezing all traffic coming from all adjacent union areas. With truck companies highly fragmented and extremely competitive, the union could always depend on some truckers signing union contracts to gain a temporary advantage over their rivals. This done, all truckers would sign because none had the financial resources necessary to weather a long strike. As national trucking companies developed, Hoffa pressed for standard wage contracts which could be administered from the Washington, D.C. headquarters. This took autonomy and power away from local city Teamster officials.

Through this and diverse other practices which depended both on the national interlocking nature of trucking and the fragmentation of trucking companies, Hoffa welded an increasingly centralized Teamsters Union (Brown 1971). It is interesting to ask what Hoffa's career might have been had he got into the Detroit carpenters local rather than the Teamsters. Being bright, articulate, hard working, and aggressive, he might have built the Detroit local into a powerful private kingdom. But because of the wholly local nature of the construction industry he would not have had the leverage necessary to build a strong centralized national union.

ORGANIZING CALIFORNIA AGRICULTURAL WORKERS

While most other American workers have enjoyed the protection of the National Labor Relations Act and minimum wage legislation in their efforts to organize unions and bargain collectively with management for a generation, agricultural workers are still beyond the protection of these laws. Several unions including the Teamsters and the United Packing House Workers have tried, without success, to organize California's agricultural workers since World War II, but the United Farm Workers Organizing Committee (UFWOC) led by César Chávez has been much more successful in recent years.

A review of its efforts provides the chance to see the importance of government policies, industry technology, and ideological factors in forming unions. Union organization drives have always raised emotions on all sides, and the California undertaking is no exception. Most discussions have been one-sided (*Barron's Weekly* August 5, 1968:1; Healy 1969; Mattheissen, 1969). The discussion which follows draws primarily on a recent book by London and Anderson (1970) and on material collected and analyzed by Claire L. Peterson (1970).

Government Support of Corporate Agriculture. Since the Spanish missions utilized local Indians as field laborers, California has had a tradition of large-scale plantations. The policies of the federal government have done much to perpetuate large-scale farming at the expense of owner-operated family farming. First, for a century the government has encouraged legal entry and turned a blind eye to illegal entry of a succession of Asians and Latin Americans to work in the fields. This continually refilled pool of unskilled workers has made possible the social technology described below.

Second, government-sponsored research has developed varieties of crops requiring complex and expensive machine technologies. These machines require much hand labor but are beyond the financial means of family farmers. Third, the federal government has developed a large system of dams and canals to bring water to the fertile but arid lands of southern California. Water costing the government fourteen dollars per acre-foot is sold to the farmers at $7.50 per acre-foot. This amounts to a subsidy of $30 million a year, and the value of the land is increased many times over by the availability of this cheap water. When the water was first made available, it was intended that these substantial subsidies would go only to family farmers, those owning 160 acres or less, who worked their own land. In fact these limitations have not been imposed, and it has been estimated by agricultural economists that at least 900,000 acres of California land held by large corporate growers receive the cheap water in violation of the 160 acre limitation (London and Anderson 1970:3–5).

Finally, a number of federal subsidies, acreage limitations, and tax measures have been enacted in order to control agricultural production and protect the family farmer, but these have all had the effect of furthering the development of absentee and large-scale farming (Mills 1951:15–20; *Barron's Weekly* August 5, 1968:3; London and Anderson 1970:3, 188). As a striking example, in 1970 one farmer in San Joaquin Valley received $4,400,000 from the United States government for *not* growing cotton (Schorr 1971a:28). What is more, this payment was possible because of numerous technical loopholes in the law which had set a $55,000 limit on subsidies available to each farmer. In a number of ways the government has facilitated the growth of corporate farming while intending to help family farming.

Social Technology. Farms are operated so workers with little skill are required in great numbers for short periods of time to perform physically taxing tasks under hot, dusty, and sometimes insecticide contaminated field conditions. To accommodate this widely fluctuating demand for labor, a pattern of migratory labor has developed for workers who follow the ripening crops from area to area; workers live in migrant camps on the plantation or in special shanty towns (MacGregor 1969; Graves 1970).

While California growers have paid wages at or above the minimum hourly rates in recent years, and whereas conditions for farm workers are better in California than any other state except Hawaii (Ramire 1969), work is sporadic and the average *annual* family income for farm workers in California is only $1600, or one-fifth the annual income of automobile or steel workers (C. Peterson 1970). Since the time of the Spanish plantations, owners have maintained a paternalistic policy toward their workers (Rushing 1968). This attitude is exemplified by the comment of owner Allan Grant, president of the California Farm Bureau Federation and member of the University of California Board of Regents, explaining to the press why there was no need for unions in California agriculture: ". . .my Philippino boys can come to my back door any time they have a problem and discuss it with me" (London and Anderson 1970:18).

For a hundred years workers have left this plantation system of agriculture with its unstable employment, low wages, and paternalism as soon as other job opportunities were available. Rather than changing the social technology of agriculture to induce workers to remain, plantation owners have sought out and imported new recruits of diverse nationalities, including Chinese, Japanese, Philippinos, and Mexicans, among others. The only break with the policy of recruiting peasants came during the depression of the 1930s when growers attracted and employed thousands of dispossessed small farmers from Nebraska, Kansas, and Oklahoma. These "Okies," though often near starvation, repeatedly rebelled against the poor working conditions. Much public attention was focused on the issues, and a general reform of the social technology was being formulated when World War II brought defense plant work to the Okies. The government then began to actively import contract laborers from Mexico to take the Okies place in the fields, thus perpetuating the social technology based on migrant peasant labor. Yet as London and Anderson (1970:61) note, there is nothing inevitable about the social technology based on peasant laborers, rather, "A peculiar type of agriculture evolved to fit the kind of labor supply already at hand, and once a vested interest in large-scale, labor-intensive agriculture developed, it tended to rationalize and perpectuate itself."

Orthodox Unionization. During the 1950s, there were several unsuccessful attempts to organize the California agricultural workers by conventional labor union techniques. The organizers did not have the protection of labor laws available in all manufacturing industries so they could not get union representation elections. What is more, the growers could fire union members, enjoin picketing, hire strike-breaking workers in Mexico and other states, and prevent organizers from talking to workers, all "unfair labor practices" according to the usual canons of labor law. As a result, a great deal of the unions" funds as well as the energies of its organizers were deflected into court battles in defense of their own activities.

The physical size of farms and the traditional practice of housing workers on the premises did much to frustrate union organizers. Growers could prevent organizers from having any contact with workers, and those living on the premises might not even be aware that a unionization drive was in progress. Again the dispersion of workers made picket lines ineffective, and when set up along secondary roads picket lines were extremely vulnerable to physical tactics by growers on isolated unionists.

The threat of violence by growers was heightened by the fact that local law enforcement agencies were more sympathetic to growers than to "foreign" migrant workers. Ethnic rivalries also served to frustrate unionization. Men of one ethnic group often scabbed against strikers of another. Organizers from factories and mills of the Midwest were not readily trusted by workers, because they and the unions they represented could withdraw at any time, abandoning the workers.

While direct efforts to unionize workers failed, another tactic used effectively in Hawaii was possible. Longshoremen there unionized pineapple and other agricultural workers decades ago by simply refusing to ship crops to the mainland until growers recognized the agricultural union. In California the Teamsters Union was in a comparable strategic position, because it could have refused to truck perishable crops to markets until agricultural unions were recognized. But throughout most of this period the Teamsters Union did not aid the organization of field workers, because it had an agreement with industry interests to favor the IBT in the unionization of cannery workers. Recently some growers have *asked* the Teamsters to unionize agricultural workers, thereby hoping to forestall unionization by the more militant union headed by César Chávez (London and Anderson 1970:155).

La Causa. In the mid-1960s a farm worker unionizing effort began which was different in three major ways from the ones just described. First, it was founded and led by Spanish-speaking Americans who were themselves farm workers, rather than professional labor unionists or radical intellectuals. Most notable of these "grassroots" organizers is César Chávez, head of the United Farm Workers Organizing Committee (UFWOC).

Second, organizers have focused not only on money issues—wages, hours, seniority rights, retirement benefits, and the like—but have been equally concerned with broader issues which challenge the peasant system of social technology and paternalism. For this reason, the growers see Chávez as a revolutionary and his followers talk of *nuestra causa,* our movement.

Third, UFWOC has been dedicated to nonviolent strategies of organization and confrontation with growers, ideas drawn from the activities of Gandhi, Martin Luther King, Jr., and Saul Alinsky. The commitment to nonviolence is based on the knowledge that conventional union tactics in California usually end in violence which is invariably blamed on unions (*Time* July 4, 1969:16–21; London and Anderson 1970:148–96; Henninger 1970). What is more, court litigation following violence has been extremely expensive and has turned public opinion *against* the union cause.

By contrast, the commitment to build a nonviolent social movement seeking human dignity and social justice gained the sympathy and support of civil rights leaders, liberal political figures, and the national news media. In addition, it brought hundreds of students and churchmen to work as volunteers with the UFWOC and induced millions of people to support the consumer boycott of grapes which cut grape consumption enough over a three-year period to convince grape growers finally to sign a labor union contract with the Chávez union.

This section of the chapter opened by showing the role of the federal government in fostering corporate agriculture in California. In recent years, the government has aided the growers in their struggle against the UFWOC and grape boycott. Department of Agriculture subsidies have helped growers compensate for strike and boycott losses. Immigration services have given large numbers of Mexican nationals visas to work in the vineyards, although federal regulations explicitly prohibit the importation of workers as strikebreakers. Federally sponsored projects, organized to train community action leaders and provide legal service to the rural poor, have been closed because some of their efforts were devoted to aiding Chávez. Finally the Department of Defense greatly increased its purchases of grapes during the boycott. In the preboycott year of 1967 it purchased seven million pounds of grapes; in the boycott year of 1969 it more than doubled its purchase to sixteen million pounds (C. Peterson 1970).

Chapter 5

INDIVIDUALS IN THE CRUCIBLE

It is faddish in some intellectual circles to bemoan the alienating conditions of modern life in which the individual loses much control over his own destiny. In the writings which take this approach, the *documented* travails of today are usually compared with an *idealized* picture of feudalism (Ellul 1964) or nineteenth century small-town American life (Mills 1951). Yet the candid accounts of the lot of common people in earlier eras of Western society give quite a different view. They make it abundantly clear that the average man in industrial society today enjoys greater freedom from privation, disease, fear of occult powers, and the arbitrary actions of those in power than the common people of any earlier era.

At the same time, people today may still *feel* more powerless and estranged than their counterparts of an earlier era. Several factors help to account for these feelings of alienation. Many jobs are dull and uncreative, but what is more important, people increasingly feel they deserve something better (Taviss 1969). General education and the belief in equal opportunity for all have raised the level of material and cultural expectations. Traditional ideological rationalizations of inequality, such as fatalism, caste, and religion, which legitimated the differences between the privileged and the common man have lost much of their power to mollify discontent.

While it has become conventional to castigate Red, Black, and the New Left radicals for stirring disaffection with the old values, it is probably true that the daily fare of television, showing the sorts of material possessions and way of life that should be enjoyed by everyone, has done more to raise the expectations of disadvantaged Whites and Blacks than all of the purportedly seditious speeches of supposed militants. There is a special irony here, for the commercial aspects of television so despised by radical intellectuals may well have a more profound revolutionary effect than all radical agitation (Daniels and Kitano 1970:119).

This chapter more than any other reflects the classical interests of industrial sociology. It begins by exploring the diverse meanings of the term alienation in an industrial situation, then describes three major strategies that managers have used in trying to compensate for worker alienation. The chapter concludes with an exploration of why high levels of alienation have not led to open rebellion against industrialism on the part of blue-collar workers, Blacks, or white-collar functionaries.

Work and Its Discontents

Here we will illustrate the sources of alienation in contemporary work, discuss some problems encountered in measuring alienation, and explore the causes of alienation by focusing on taxicab drivers.

Alienating Work

Most of the late eighteenth century ideologists of the Industrial Revolution saw the machine-paced factory system of production as a teacher of morals and a cure for laziness. Jeremy Bentham, for example, proposed to construct a building that would be half prison and half factory, designed "for grinding rogues honest and idle men industrious" (Bell 1960:228). Economists sometimes still see repetitive factory work as having this virtue. Alfred Marshall (1948:258) describes a mass production screw-making machine and concludes, "The person who minds it must have an intelligence and an energetic sense of responsibility, which goes a long way toward making a fine character." Adam Smith, starting from the assumption that a man's identity is formed in his work, foresaw in 1776 quite a different consequence of industrial factory work. Rather than seeing it as a device for teaching morals and industriousness, he saw that the division of labor made possible by factory mechanization would make much work trivial, repetitive, and dull and he feared the consequences that this would have on workers. Thus, Adam Smith, the father of laissez faire economics, was also the father of alienation studies. Karl Marx, writing seventy years later, drew heavily on Smith's perspective in developing his theory of alienated labor (Hoselitz 1964).

Most of the founders of contemporary sociology from Durkheim and

Weber to Simmel and Pareto have dealt with Marx's alienation idea in one way or another. All the various usages of the term have been gathered and distilled into five "variants" of alienation by Melvin Seeman (1959). His summary comprises a convenient framework for talking about alienation in contemporary work even though he did not form the classification with particular reference to work situations.

Powerlessness. The first variant of alienation Seeman discusses is *powerlessness;* it refers to the degree of control a worker has over the details of the job he performs. The classical craftsman and professional would be low on this dimension of alienation because they have control. Assembly line workers and textile mill machine-tenders would be quite high, because the pace of work, the specific sequence of tasks, and the quality of work produced are largely predetermined by the machine system itself (Blauner 1964; Fullan 1970). The low level white-collar bureaucrat tied by rigid rules to particular procedures experiences much the same powerlessness (Perlin 1962; Ritti 1971). Under such conditions, it is not easy to feel any pride in workmanship.

Meaninglessness. The second variant is *meaninglessness;* here the employee sees no clear connection between the tasks he performs and the final output of the organization. An automobile worker knows he is working on a component for an automobile, but in many industries workers do not see how their efforts fit into the whole process. The "electrolitic condenser core winders" in a factory where I worked one summer during the Korean War knew that they were employed in a "defense plant" for they had to have a special badge to be admitted. Yet they had no notion that the delicate windings they produced fit into the radar for navy carrier aircraft. They worked to meet production quotas completely *unaware* that the substandard windings they regularly produced, inspected, and sent on might cause a failure leading to the loss of a military aircraft and its pilot. Bureaucratic settings where there is no clear relationship between the tasks a functionary must perform and the larger goals of the organization often foster meaninglessness.

Normlessness. This third variant of alienation, *normlessness,* does not mean a literal lack of all norms but rather a *structured confusion* of norms. In work situations it involves the use of illegal or prohibited means to achieve a legitimate goal (Bensman 1967; Hellerstein 1963). It is structured in that there may be no effective or efficient legitimate means available so illegitimate means are required. The root notion of normlessness is captured by the statement, "You can't run a railroad within the law." As another case in point, police rationalize their use of "brutality" as the only effective way to maintain "law and order" as Westley (1953) has shown. The "cop on the beat" knows that his superiors expect and, in effect, require him to use violence; at the same time, he knows that he will be reprimanded and perhaps fired by the same superiors if he is publicly caught in the act of using violence. Bureaucratic functionaries such as welfare workers and teachers are often forced by the pressure of their heavy work loads to employ actions which if not violent are equally destructive of their clients' interests (May 1964).

Many blue-collar workers know their work is shoddy, but while the foremen may talk about maintaining standards, he only urges them to do *more* rather than do *better* work. A dramatic illustration of this double standard is provided by Bensman and Gerver (1963). They describe an airplane-wing assembly shop in a factory employing 2600 workers under United States Air Force contract. The skin of each wing is fastened to the frame using "stop nuts" which prevent the bolts from vibrating loose under the extreme stress of flight. Due to slight errors in construction, skin and frame holes often do not exactly line up. A "tap," a very simple tool, can be used to correct the alignment but its use destroys the effectiveness of the stop nuts, thus endangering the strength of the wing. The Air Force prohibits the use of taps and the mere possession of a tap in the factory is grounds for dismissal. However, workers, foremen, and even company inspectors all conspire in their regular use, and a great deal of time and ingenuity is expended in not getting caught by Air Force inspectors. Workers may enjoy this game just as, at some level, police may enjoy using violence, and case workers may relish frustrating their clients, but these behaviors engender normlessness (Pugh 1966).

Robert K. Merton (1968: Chs. 8, 19) shows two common structural conditions that make for normlessness among white-collar workers. The first is a product of bureaucratic rule-tropism as mentioned in Chapter 3. The contemporary white-collar functionary is rewarded for following the rules of his job. Thus, he is unmotivated to modify his job performance in response to changing exigencies. Merton calls this sort of rigidity "trained incapacity," in recognition of the fact that the incapacity is derived not from individual ineptitude but from the bureaucratic structuring of jobs.

Merton's second example of conditions which make for normlessness among white-collar workers is a trained incapacity derived from technical expertise itself. One characteristic of technical and engineering training is its concentration in a specific subject area (Perrucci and Gerstl 1969). This narrow focus is carried over into the ways technical jobs tend to be structured. Projects having to do with routing a highway through a city, developing a weapons system, making a better automobile are subdivided into a number of delimited technical questions. It becomes, by default, no one's responsibility to look at the social, ecological, and political consequences of the total enterprise.

Isolation. The fourth variant of alienation is *isolation,* the most difficult to characterize for it is often found combined with the others. Alienating isolation occurs when an individual lives a double life, the one defined in strongly held convictions, the other in the realities of a day-to-day existence. This is the alienation of intellectuals, revolutionaries, and many teenagers. It can be found in many situations above the blue-collar level. Many staff personnel feel a strain between their own values and the work in which they are involved. During the 1960s, for example, as many as 10 percent of all United Airline stewardesses married, although this was then against company regulations. One stewardess who lived a double life as a United Airline stewardess and the wife of a Florida attorney for four years, reports that her superiors did not object when for years the same young man answered her apartment phone. "As long as they thought I was just *living* with a man, everything was all right," but she was summarily fired for "misconduct" when her marriage was discovered!

Scientists and engineers working for corporations often face the dilemma of working toward scientific goals on the one hand and following organizational directives on the other. At the very time in 1968 that automobile engineers were pointing with understandable pride to the fact that they had devised pollution-control devices good and economical enough to meet 1970 federal automobile air pollution guidelines, automobile company management was testifying before the United States Congress that such guidelines would be impossible to meet (*Wall Street Journal,* February 20, 1968). In our increasingly research-oriented industries this disparity between the technically *possible* and the currently *practiced* will heighten the alienation of isolation.

Self-Estrangement. The final variant of alienation defined by Seeman is *self-estrangement.* Alienation from one's "self" is a simple metaphor but it is always in danger of becoming purely metaphysical in use (Taviss 1969). Self-estrangement is most clearly seen in practice in those sales and service occupations in which the *appearance* of "charm," "character," "honesty," and the like, is central to successful job performance. Here the person makes an instrument of his own personality and body. William H. Whyte (1956) explores this hollow character in his book *The Organizational Man* and C. Wright Mills (1951) pursues a similar diagnosis in *White Collar;* their view of the relationship between bureaucracy and alienation is given considerable support by Aiken and Hage (1966) and Bonjean and Grimes (1970). The best characterization of self-estrangement is still Willie Loman, the central character in Arthur Miller's play, *Death of a Salesman.*

MEASURING ALIENATION

According to the theorists from Adam Smith and Karl Marx to Erich Fromm, Jacques Ellul, and Herbert Marcuse, alienation is supposed to have a wide range of consequences for the affected individual. Finding work unfulfilling, he may throw himself into the escapist pursuits of sex, alcohol, sadism, and gambling; he may withdraw from an active political and community life to the less demanding environment of the home; or, he may turn to aggressively attack the system which generates his alienation.

A set of studies over the past fifteen years has attempted to probe the consequences of alienation. The studies tend to conclude that alienation from work does not have the dire consequences predicted (cf. Seeman 1967; Neal and Rettig 1963)! These results are quite surprising until one notes that these authors have changed the meaning of alienation by the measures they use to study the process. The researchers typically ask workers whether they feel alienated; thus, alienation in their usage is a *subjective* feeling state. The theorists of alienation however were referring to the *objective* conditions of the work situation as illustrated in the section above; we will call this *objective alienation*. From the perspective of the theorists, an alienated individual may very likely *not* be able to accurately diagnose his condition as alienation.

The Career of the Alienation Concept. The focus of American sociology since World War II on the survey measurement of individual attitudes has left relatively unexplored the measurement of social structures such as objective alienation (Etzioni 1968; Taviss 1969). While the effects of *objective* alienation are essentially unknown the fragmented information now available is suggestive (Friedmann 1955; Neff 1968). For example, the causes of death for men in the prime years of employment, twenty to sixty-four, vary widely by occupation. In some instances, high death rates are caused by work hazards rather than alienation; thus, mine workers have exceedingly high death rates due to tuberculosis brought on by inhaling minute dust particles in a damp environment over a number of years; they also show a much higher rate of death due to industrial accidents. Death from alcoholism, ulcers, and suicide on the other hand may be related to the alienating conditions of work. Professionals and craftsmen who are relatively free from alienating conditions show low death rates due to such causes, while guards, police, and salesmen show high death rates due to duodenal ulcers, and managers show comparatively high rates of death by cirrhosis of the liver, a by-product of alcoholism (Rushing 1968; Tuckman 1969). Such data as these are gross in at least two respects; first, the occupational categories often combine specific jobs of high and low alienation. Second, other variables that may influence death rates have not been taken into account. Managers may be older on the average than other workers, and cirrhosis of the liver is relatively infrequent in young persons.

Most studies, designed to tap the consequences of objective alienation in a range of specific work settings, have used reports by workers of job satisfaction as the measure of job satisfaction. The studies do show that professionals such as doctors and lawyers report much greater job satisfaction than assembly line workers (Blauner 1960; Wilensky 1964b), but studies comparing various sorts of blue-collar occupations do not show a close correlation between the two sorts of alienation. Blauner (1964) for example, has found that textile workers who experience high objective alienation do not express dissatisfaction with their jobs. His explanation is that various social and cultural factors in the isolated communities where textile mills are located compensate for objective alienation. This explanation is given further support by Form (1969) who has studied assembly line auto workers in four different cultures. Though the level of objective alienation is the same in these four settings, the expectations of workers are quite different and thus their felt alienation varies greatly. Such studies suggest that the effect of objective alienation is often obscured (Rushing 1971). Studies that can show how to eliminate the effects of nontechnological factors are needed.

An exploratory study which attempts to control the effects of nontechnological factors is currently being pursued by this author and David Johnson. We are interested in the effect of work on marital stability (the best measure of subjective alienation available in the data). Using United States census data we have isolated thirty specific blue-collar work situations which should theoretically show varying degrees of objective alienation, and we have statistically controlled the effects of income, geographical region, race, education, and several other variables. Our preliminary findings suggest there are wide differences in the degree of marital stability among various blue-collar jobs and in most instances these differences seem linked to the exigencies of job life.

A study by Mead (1969) suggests the importance of objective alienation for rates of productivity (another possible indirect measure of subjective alienation). He compares the productivity of the two major kinds of farms in the Soviet Union. State farms are organized along standard bureaucratic lines with workers taking no direct part in decision processes. By contrast collective farms are organized so that all workers participate in the management of the farm enterprise. Solid evidence from Russian sources is fragmentary but where meaningful comparisons can be made, it is clear that in the more alienating conditions of the state farms productivity is much lower than on the more free collective farms. These data are most perplexing to Soviet leaders who, for ideological as well as managerial reasons, would like to eliminate the collective farms entirely.

ALIENATION AND JOB SATISFACTION AMONG TAXICAB DRIVERS

The link between subjective and objective alienation has been most clearly demonstrated in studies of specific technologies (Blauner 1964; Fullan 1970). We will examine the case of taxicab drivers studied by Kirk Elifson and the author, because the driver's situation highlights the principal factors involved. We found that these low paid, low skilled (*Occupational Outlook* 1969:379) and low prestige (Hodge, Siegel, and Rossi 1964) workers, *unlike* most workers at comparable blue-collar job levels report very great job satisfaction. In fact, their level of subjective alienation was as low as many of the free professionals and markedly lower than that of blue-collar workers generally (Blauner 1960).

The study evaluated several alternative explanations for the low subjective level of alienation among cabbies and found the primary explanation in the low levels of objective alienation which they experienced. Numerous cab drivers working for a large company as well as those who own their own cab told us in effect "I am my own boss" and in many ways they are (Backes 1969). Their job freedom is particularly striking when compared with the blue-collar factory jobs which are their alternative sources of employment (Meissner 1969).

Job Freedom. The objective freedom of taxicab drivers can be seen in a number of ways: unlike most workers who stand at one station in a factory, drivers are mobile throughout an entire metropolitan area; they are free of close supervision, thus are able to set the pace of their own work; even for a few minutes they hold persons of higher income and prestige in their power; by a multitude of ingenious techniques, both legal and illegal, they can work to increase their income; their jobs are full of danger and in response cabbies have developed a protective fraternity which cuts across other allegiances: as one of our respondents said, "A cabdriver's a cabdriver whether a guy is from another company or not, if he drives a cab, we'll help him, Negro or white" (Elifson 1968:14); and finally, driving provides a greater variety of job experiences than almost any other blue-collar job. Many cabbies noted that "You never know what the next run will bring," and then launched into a wild tale of adventure or human folly.

The conditions of low objective alienation just described are inherent in the way the taxi business is organized, but other factors in the environment may also provide more or less job freedom. At the time the study was conducted, conditions in the city increased job freedom. Unemployment was so low that taxi companies had to hire anyone they could find, including many with extensive criminal records; companies could not afford to penalize or fire drivers who ignored the many rules which were designed to increase company control over drivers. One of the primary means of control over drivers was the dispatcher who communicated with drivers by a radio telephone. While he was supposed to order drivers anywhere in the city to pick up customers, dispatchers often had to beg drivers to take assignments which were undesirable for one reason or another. Thus, the short-term conditions of low unemployment had the effect of increasing the job freedoms that were already inherent in the job.

While most blue-collar technologies do not naturally provide the degree of job freedom available to taxicab drivers, managers have paid some attention to redesigning jobs to reduce objective alienation, a process called "job enlargement." Much greater attention has been placed on compensating for alienation. It is to such strategies that we now turn.

Overcoming Alienation

Numerous different strategies have been devised by businessmen, engineers, lawyers, and social scientists to induce employees to work enthusiastically. In spite of the variety, most fit within one or another of the three major approaches which we will discuss here: the first, scientific management—compensates for; the second, human relations—accommodates to; and the third, the rule of law—tries to overcome objective alienation. While scientific management and human relations were developed partially by engineers and social scientists to forestall union organization and to represent modern forms of paternalism (as defined in Chapter 2), the rule of law has evolved out of union-management negotiations since the 1930s and represents a modern form of fraternalism.

Scientific Management

In the past when technologies only demanded the *physical* labor of workers, as in the building of the pyramids of Egypt or in plantation agriculture, slave laborers were sufficiently efficient. Given more complex machine technology, it is important that workers have a positive attitude toward their work because they must exercise skill and judgment. The momentary inattention of a single oil refinery worker or airplane mechanic, for example, may cost the corporation hundreds of thousands of dollars. It has thus become essential for management to pay attention to worker motivation.

The early industrial manufacturers preached a gospel of diligent effort; this sort of ideological incentive was not too effective because manufacturers were not able to manipulate the divine reward structure. At the beginning of this century the engineers who had been instrumental in creating the technology of mass production turned their attention to the worker whose craft skill had been made obsolete by the new technology. Frederick Taylor was foremost among these human engineers whose techniques came to be called "scientific management." He was aware of the alienating consequences of trivial work tasks in mass production. In order to encourage the worker's full cooperation and interest in doing good work, he proposed compensating the worker for complying with management-established routines by an increase of 30 to 100% over his ordinary wages. The increased wages were to be given as "incentive pay," based on the amount of work the individual actually produced. In this way, Taylor reasoned, workers would be motivated to work diligently in order to gain higher wages.

American managers were very impressed with scientific management and many began to pay workers according to the number of units of work produced per day, a strategy called the piecework incentive plan. Taylor's ideas were admired in other countries as well. V. I. Lenin, architect of the Communist Revolution in Russia, implemented a piecework incentive plan in Russian factories, and all industrializing nations, both capitalist and communist, now use a combination of ideological and monetary incentives to motivate workers.

While piecework incentives have been a dominant philosophy of American industrial engineers for the last fifty years, the overall proportion of production and related workers participating in individual and group incentive plans has remained relatively constant, just under 30 percent since the end of World War II. Although industry tradition seems to be an important factor and regional variation is evident, piecework incentive plans are prevalent under two different sets of conditions. The first occurs where technology is relatively primitive, labor costs are high relative to other costs, and job security is slight. The second takes place where technology is highly sophisticated but where a few workers can block production. Here incentive is paid not to increase the rate of work but to maximize machine utilization. Examples of the first type of industry include apparel, cigar, and leather work; examples of the latter include the steel industries, knitting mills, and the manufacture of electronic equipment.

Incentive Plans Under Attack. The effectiveness of these plans to motivate workers has become the focus of much critical attention in recent years. Piecework incentives have come under attack for two related reasons, and each of them bears directly on the principles of scientific management. First, workers who have been taught by scientific management that they were employed to produce rather than to think have turned their creative capacities to beating the incentive system itself. Acting very much like the "economic men" Taylor assumed them to be, workers in most instances have found they can maximize their own long-term earnings by producing much less than they could (Roy 1952; Peterson and Rath 1964). As a result the incentive system has become a central source of dispute among work groups and a grievance against management rather than the focal point of worker-manager cooperation Taylor hoped it would be (Behrend 1959).

Piecework incentives are criticized for a second reason. Taylor and his followers believed that incentive pay would make the worker responsive to management advice on the best way to do a job; this would make the worker receptive to technological change. In practice quite the opposite has been the case. Workers are reluctant to change accustomed job routines because a change would mean, at least temporarily, a reduction in incentive earnings. Thus, the piecework incentive system has become a block in the way of technological change.

Over the years many white-collar jobs in sales have been converted to a piecework system usually called commissions. Most automobile salesmen receive a small base pay and are then paid an additional percentage on auto sales made. Incentive pay systems will probably continue to flourish among such salesmen but will become less important in blue-collar automated technologies where individual workers do not produce discrete items but participate as part of a group in complex continuous processes. Under such conditions piecework incentives become meaningless and perhaps unnecessary, for more powerful incentives have been reintroduced into the work process as we will show.

Human Relations

While scientific management takes an engineering attitude toward the worker and asserts an economic basis of motivation, a different tack has been taken by Elton Mayo and his followers at the Harvard School of Business Administration (Bendix and Fisher 1949). They take a clinical role toward the worker and assume a psychological basis of worker motivation. This strategy has been called "human relations" in industry. The best recent summaries of this position are found in Katz and Kahn (1966) and Strauss (1968).

The early studies in this tradition found that when workers were given the *feeling* that they were participating in managerial decisions and were made to *feel* part of a larger work team, they responded with higher productivity and lower absenteeism (Morse and Reimer 1956). This seemed like a panacea for management; productivity could be increased with an expenditure of nothing more than charm! The long-termed effects of this strategy have been a disappointment to management for several reasons.

First, the results of the early studies have been challenged. It has been found that in some instances the higher productivity was a function of the increased surveillance over workers during the study, and not a product of management's more human approach. Other studies have shown that worker productivity is very poorly associated with attitudes toward management, job satisfaction, morale, and the like (Herzberg, Mausner, and Snyderman 1959; Vroom 1964; Opshal and Dunnette 1966; Carey 1967).

Second, the more humane way of treating workers must be *real* to be effective. Where management only *appears* to give workers decision-making power, the hypocrisy itself becomes the focus of added worker disaffection. Telephone workers I interviewed in Illinois were particularly bitter toward the management of the Bell Telephone Company because it treated them in ways they saw as arbitrary and self-serving; at the same time the company presented a public relations facade as kindly "Ma Bell."

When the human relations approach extends its concern for the worker beyond the plant gates into the recreational and civic activities of the community, it then is a new form of paternalism (as in Chapter 2). This new paternalism is found in many work settings and is highly developed where many semiskilled women are employed to perform delicate jobs as in the manufacture of electronics components. It is also highly developed in companies which have decided to resist the unionization of their workers. In the highly unionized steel industry, one of the largest firms has developed a complex human relations program in the successful effort to avoid unionization. The company asserts that it gives its workers all the benefits that the union has won elsewhere and more beside. Management is willing to pay the higher costs of paternalism in order to maintain its freedom from union domination. Quite often management has embraced the human relations approach to avoid unionization. Thus, paternalism and fraternalism are still counterposed as managerial strategies in the twentieth century.

THE RULE OF LAW

There have been numerous developments in industrial relations. Most of them have been viewed by experts in the field as extensions of the human relations approach (Katz and Kahn 1966), but a distinctly different basis of defining the organization-worker relationship has been developing. Its basic assumption is that employees will work conscientiously for an organization which they feel treats them justly. This approach to industrial relations has no single name but since its view of man and society derives from legal thinking, we will call it "the rule of law" in organizations.

Managers of all eras have claimed to treat their workers justly. Two factors distinguish the rule of law orientation: first, each of the parties— labor, management, and unions—stand as equals under the law, having clearly defined rights and obligations; second, each party can seek redress through a specified set of procedures when it feels its rights have been infringed. In legal language this is called "the due process of law." It has two aspects which are useful to distinguish, *procedural* due process—the set of laws and procedures for regularly hearing claims, and *substantive* due process—the system operating effectively to obtain justice (Selznick 1969).

Advocates of the rule of law approach suggest that it forms the framework within which the bitter conflicts between management and labor can be transformed into cooperative discussions over the means of mutually achieving long-term objectives (Peterson 1966). Several factors mitigate against this goal being fully reached. First, the rules may be unilaterally promulgated and administered, a mock rule of law; second, management and union may have to maintain a bellicose public stance to please stockholders and workers, respectively. Each of these possibilities is illustrated below.

Two Kinds of Plans. Many large bureaucratically structured organizations such as the federal Civil Service, United States Army, and Catholic Church have long had systems of procedural due process by which employees can question the directives given by their superiors. All of these plans employ judges who are part of the organization and who thus are directly responsible to management itself; in fact, management is defendant, judge, and jury (Scott 1965). In practice such appeals systems usually do not satisfy either the felt injustices of individual workers or operate as mechanisms within which needed reform can be generated (Evan 1962). Thus, these systems of procedural due process have not in practice made for substantive due process.

The rule of law for blue-collar workers in industrial organizations has not been unilaterally promulgated by management as it was in the sorts of organizations just discussed. Rather, it has emerged since the 1930s out of the conflictful struggles between management, workers, and labor unions in which the federal government has played an important role. The National Labor Relations Act of 1934 forms the cornerstone of the rule of law in industry. Through it industrial workers throughout the nation gained the right to organize labor unions and to collectively bargain with management over wages, hours, and working conditions (Falcone 1962). Thus, what had often been a bloody struggle to organize workers into unions became more nearly a contest between management and unions to attract the loyalty of workers with the National Labor Relations Board (NLRB) operating as referee to see that neither side intimidated workers. Besides setting the rules and acting as referee the government may be called upon to mediate and arbitrate differences between the various parties.

Today, union representation elections have largely replaced the bombings, goon squards, industrial sabotage, labor spies, strike breakers of an earlier era (Pelling 1960). Over the years, there has developed a system of rules and procedures forming a framework within which the power contest between various parties can be decided without resorting to violence.

At issue has been the union's right to negotiate wages, seniority rights, work quotas, pension rights, and related working conditions (Vollmer 1960). But in recent years wider issues of equity have emerged such as the extent to which workers with seniority in one plant of a firm have a right to good jobs in a new plant being built by that firm in a distant location.

While the discussion of such matters was first seen as a power struggle between union and management, continuous discussion has tended to shift the focus to wider questions of equity and each party has come to recognize that its own interest is best served when the other party is prospering and satisfied. The further development of such labor-management cooperation on the basis of mutually understood equities is largely prevented by the larger social context within which negotiations typically take place. Corporation managers are expected by profit minded shareholders to keep wages as low as possible, while workers expect their elected union representatives to get every possible penny in raises. Thus an atmosphere of hostile antagonism is fostered and perpetuated by union and management to satisfy the expectations of each side. The staging of this polemical drama prevents the rule of law from becoming the basis for more creative labor management relations.

Individual Rights. As general conditions of work have improved over recent decades, the rule of law strategy has increasingly been applied to equities for individual employees. The problems are much the same—wages, seniority, and the like—but the procedures for guaranteed procedural due process of individual grievances vary widely from one firm to another. The system developed in the automobile industry between General Motors and the United Auto Workers is a good example. The worker with a complaint discusses it with his shop steward, the man in the lowest level of the union hierarchy corresponding to the firm's foreman. If the union shop steward and the management foreman cannot settle the matter, it is referred to an appeals board representing higher levels in management and the union. Several successively higher levels of appeals boards may need to hear the case and if they cannot agree, the grievance is given to an eminent and mutually trusted professor of labor law who makes a binding settlement.

The system of procedural due process just described will be seen as equitable only so long as the union fairly represents the interests of the worker. But on many issues the union itself is an interested party or even the cause of the worker's grievance. In cognizance of this fact the National Labor Relations Act was amended in 1959 to safeguard the individual's rights against the arbitrary actions of his union. Since he must seek redress through the courts at considerable personal expense and in some cases physical danger to himself (in those instances where the union resorts to terrorizing its members), the individual union member may not enjoy substantive due process.

For the various reason just reviewed the rule of law, like scientific management and human relations, has not proved in practice to be the great boon to labor management harmony which its advocates had predicted, but each has contributed to the development of more humane and equitable labor management relations over the last half century.

The Dissipation of Revolutionary Discontent

While much of the first two parts of this chapter have looked down at the individual from management's point of view, this part looks up from the production and office floor. Karl Marx and other alienation theorists thought the condition of factory work in a capitalist society would lead workers to class consciousness and revolution (Zeitlin 1966).

While it is easy to scoff at predictions which have not come true in the 125 years since they were made, it is more instructive to see *why* the Marxian working-class revolution has not occurred.

Marx expected that the revolution would begin in the most alienated sectors of the most advanced industrial nations. His prediction has lead many sociologists to study Detroit automobile workers following World War II and ghetto Blacks since 1964 in part because objective alienation is very high in these situations. We will explore the reasons why objective alienation has not lead to open rebellion by assembly line workers, ghetto Blacks, or white-collar workers.

RATIONALIZING FAILURE

The framework and much of the data for this section comes from Eli Chinoy's *Automobile Workers and the American Dream*. Although his study was published in 1955, little has changed for automobile workers or the vast proportion of industrial workers since then (Meissner 1969; Form 1969; Marcson 1970). Chinoy finds that workers intensely dislike their work and quite realistically see no great opportunity for promotion up and out of the blue-collar ranks irrespective of how diligently and intelligently they work. But while they feel frustration they do not turn against their employer or the system at large. In spite of their own experience to the contrary they continue to espouse "the great American dream" that hard work and assertiveness can raise any man to the top in our society.

A number of different mechanisms seem to help workers maintain this belief in success while rationalizing their failure. In the first place, the general standard of living has been rising steadily since the Great Depression of the 1930s so workers can point to advances in their material well-being. Working-class families typically own color television sets, a late model automobile, a motor boat, and a vacation cottage on a lake—material possessions enjoyed by none of their grandparents. Greater material affluence has not made the worker less sensitive to economic cycles of employment and lay-off because a rapidly increasing percentage of these goods have been purchased on credit so that even brief periods of unemployment threaten the household economy and may quickly radicalize otherwise apolitical workers (*Wall Street Journal* June 25, 1968). Several strategies have been used to stabilize income. Men "moonlight" at second jobs and their wives increasingly seek employment to *ensure* the flow of material possessions into the home (Wilensky 1963). Government unemployment benefits, company efforts to stabilize the levels of employment, and unions' partially successful efforts to achieve a guaranteed annual income to stabilize family economy make workers better credit risks, and militate against their politicalization.

The workers' quest for advancement within the automobile company,

Chinoy finds, is blunted by the realization that this means becoming a fore-man, a position which is itself a deadend since management personnel is now recruited from college students not from foremen (*Wall Street Journal* December 26, 1967). Mobility is possible for the most bright and articulate workers who can advance to positions of power, prestige, and better pay by becoming part of the union apparatus. Thus, potential leaders of worker revolt are co-opted into the formal union structure. Even for those not seeking careers in the union, it still helps to siphon off discontent because workers derive great satisfaction from the fact that they have power over management through the right to strike and vicariously through the union leadership who talk man-to-man with "the bosses" (Peck 1963). What is more, the union itself may become the butt of worker discontent (Van de Vall 1970).

The average worker, having given up a quest for occupational advancement, devotes a great deal of effort and ingenuity to the achievement of more limited goals which come to be interpreted as" really getting ahead." Workers perfect work habits which satisfy their foremen with a minimum of effort (Roy, 1953). Finally, they scheme to be placed on jobs which are easier, safer, cleaner, quieter, better paying and relatively immune to un-employment (Peterson and Rath 1964). At the same time Chinoy notes that many workers define factory work as temporary, work in the factory being the means to get enough money to establish businesses—a machine shop, filling station, or turkey ranch. In practice, however, these hopes are largely utopian as few workers are able to save enough, and fewer have the talent and knowledge to make a success in the business world (Mayer and Gold-stein 1964). Most married workers turn to passive leisures—family, hobbies, spectator sports (Lever 1969), while their younger co-workers devote their energies to drinking, dating, gambling, fast automobiles, and hunting (Shostak 1969).

For all of this, most older workers will admit that they are failures, but they often say that this has been for the sake of other people. Some believe their careers were disrupted by war. Many more assert they labored hard and sacrificed much to keep a secure but relatively low-paying job rather than buy a turkey ranch with its higher risks so their children could have "all the advantages" they never had. Surveys consistently show that workers do not want their children to follow them into the plant; rather, they want more education and higher prestige jobs for their offspring (Shostak 1969). They project onto their children the guilt for their own failure, and this has become a major theme of intergenerational conflict. All too often the parental "sacrifice" is in vain, for parents have not provided the home en-vironment conducive to their children's academic and occupational achieve-ment (Shostak and Gomberg 1964: Ch. 3; Peterson and DeBord 1966).

Still, the real income of wage workers has doubled over the last two decades. Factory work has become less arduous and enough workers' sons have become accountants and doctors to sustain a belief in individual opportunity.

SCAPEGOATING POLITICS

Even when his rationalizations for failure are unsuccessful, the worker has seldom focused hostility on the capitalist-industrial *system*. He has more commonly seen its imperfections in the machinations of particular interests, be they union bosses, Negroes or their agents, the federal government, communists, intellectuals, hippies, or Jews.

Passionately attacking some convenient group as responsible for all travail rather than seeking the underlying causes of a problem is called *scapegoating*. This ideological shifting of responsibility is quite prevalent in human affairs, and attempts are often made to exploit this psychological mechanism for political or economic advantage.

Jews have been the favorite scapegoat in Europe since the establishment of Christianity as the state church of the Roman Empire. In the American industrial sphere a number of scapegoating images have been used recurrently to win the loyalty of workers and influence the opinion of the public. On one hand, union organizers are portrayed as foreign-controlled communist heathens; in labor-organizing drives in Southern Biblebelt textile mills CIO has been said to mean "Christ is Out" (Pope 1965). Where such applications are inappropriate, organizers are tabbed as corrupt gang-linked thugs (Kennedy 1960). On the other hand, owners are portrayed as profit-hungry exploiters of the righteous toiling classes, who are callous to industrial accidents and use police and imported strike breakers as unwitting instruments of oppression (Boyer and Morais 1955; Weir 1967). These epithets have only the dull ring of history in stable unionized industries, but they are renewed in every fresh organizing drive, such as the current effort to organize the California agricultural workers discussed in Chapter 4.

Such class-based scapegoating has always been more important in Europe than in America. In this country, racism aimed at potential job rivals has been more important. The other side of this scapegoating ideology has been the patriotic affirmation of community and nation against foreigners. In the past century, racist scapegoating was aimed primarily at Irish and eastern European immigrants. In this century, it has been aimed at the black immigrants from the rural South.

Alienated workers are not continuously active in community affairs and politics. They are most easily brought into active political participation only when they feel threatened and then are galvanized to action by political leaders who are able to define successfully a scapegoat for worker frustrations. Thus, alienated employees are open to demogogues of the left or of the right particularly when their material well-being is threatened. A number of studies have shown that our well-to-do workers, whether white or black, are conservative, intolerant of alternative ideas, and willing to follow authoritarian leadership (Lipset 1960; Aiken, Ferman, and Sheppard 1968; Lipset and Raab 1969).

We will focus on Blacks in the next section; here we focus on scapegoating by regularly employed white workers. Since World War II this group has enjoyed almost continuous high levels of employment and newfound affluence. In the late 1960s, however, this group felt its security threatened by the uncertainties of the near future (*Wall Street Journal* June 25, 1968, October 18, 1968). Very little questioning of the complex industrializing processes took place; rather, a scapegoating logic developed which could have made race war in America. The chances of this occurring may be slight but the potential is well worth examining.

Scapegoating Cycle. The scapegoating logic cycle of white workers is as follows: the purchasing power of income is cut by inflation which is caused in large part by various federal spending policies, including federal spending on foreign aid, the poverty programs, and other welfare measures. Note that no cognizance is taken of the fact that most of the federal dollar goes to expenditures for war and war preparation; the great reluctance of working men to advocate cutting these expenditures comes in part from the fact that war-work provides millions of jobs. What is more, workers press their elected representatives toward belligerent national goals out of a strong feeling of belonging to something powerful—the strongest country on earth. Thus, cuts in federal spending must come from the non-defense related sector.

Foreign aid is viewed by workers as strengthening other nations economically so that they can import goods to the United States, thus creating unemployment here. Welfare is identified as aid to unemployed Blacks who will either swell welfare roles with high birth rates or become competitors for jobs. The government pressure for school and residential desegregation is seen as forcing Blacks into working-class white suburbs, while the well-to-do suburbs remain white. The ghetto riots of the 1960s are viewed widely as products of federal government encouragement. Thus the 'war on poverty' is seen by many white workers as a war against the hard working, God fearing, patriotic, white working class (Leggett 1968).

Workers have felt without leadership or even representation in civic affairs, while they believe Blacks and Jews have become powerful because they are organized. Workers see themselves as confronted by a federal government which is the agent of these other groups. In the 1968 presidential campaign many workers originally supported Robert F. Kennedy. When he was shot, a number switched their allegiance to George Wallace, which seems strange if one focuses on the platforms of these two men; both were seen by many working people as standing for the individual against big government, big business, big unions, and faceless inhumane organizations generally (Lipset 1969; Raab 1969). For many blue-collar workers the issues involved in the Vietnam war, ghetto riots, and the revolt of youth highlight their own sense of powerlessness, meaninglessness and normlessness. Blacks, along with hippie youth, have been the most available domestic scapegoats for the working-class malaise, while the "Communist conspiracy" has served in this capacity beyond the borders of the United States (*Wall Street Journal* October 18, 1968; Weir 1967).

BLACK ALIENATION

By any measure, the level of alienation should be high among working-class Blacks. They have been the last hired and the first fired from all but the menial jobs. Before World War II the level of unemployment was marginally higher for Blacks than Whites; since that time the disparity has grown wider, (Willhelm and Powell 1964) the rate of Negro unemployment having gradually risen to *double* the white rate (*Wall Street Journal* October 24, 1968, March 9, 1970).

Another contributor to objective alienation among Blacks has been education. Numerous studies have shown that for Whites there is a close association between years of schooling and level of income. But the same studies show *no* association between levels of education and income for Blacks (cf. Blau and Duncan, 1967:239). The popularly held belief in opportunity-through-education has not benefited Blacks generally in this society.

Given the high levels of objective alienation among Blacks, subjective alienation should be high as well. Little research has been focused on their felt alienation, but there is an extensive literature on a related concept, "self-esteem." A great number of authors, Black and White, radical and conservative, have asserted that the conditions of Negro life in America have made for low self-esteem and a number of self-demeaning accommodations such as "Uncle Tomism." This literature has recently been challenged by McCarthy and Yancey (1971) who show that most available solid evidence shows that working-class Blacks do not act as if they felt alienated.

In all likelihood they employ many of the same rationalizations of "failure" discussed for white automobile workers. The existence of racial discrimination adds another major dimension to the rationalization. Put in brief, the ideological statement is, "A black brother can't make out in whitey's world of work." A number of authors have argued that it is possible to grow up in the large ghettos relatively isolated from the achievement norms of the larger society or to at least define achievement in "realistic" terms that do not make for subjective alienation. It is not easy to be sanguine about such a culture of poverty (whether it be that of ghetto Blacks, Appalachian Whites, or reservation Indians) even if one admires adaptations to adversity or merely sees them as effective "opiates" which dull revolutionary discontent. A policy of perpetuating the ghetto will foster a "reservation" system for Blacks and thus reinforce the racial caste system. Such a policy defies not only the belief in equality but also counters the pressures of the crucible of industry which is an incessant mixer of peoples.

BLACK IMMIGRANTS

Scholars who look for an alternative to the reservation system often turn to the model provided by the absorption of immigrant nationality groups into the main stream of American life (cf. Glazer and Moynihan 1970). This is "the melting pot" view. It argues that the emigration of Blacks from the rural South to the northern industrial cities during and since World War I is parallel to the emigration of foreign nationals from Europe before that time. The Negro emigration is compared with experiences of Irish, Italians, and eastern Europeans, because these groups came from peasant stock without industrial experience and settled in already well-established industrial centers, taking the least skilled jobs. Over the course of several generations they worked up the job ladder and more or less completely melded into the general population.

Like many European immigrants, Blacks came to the industrial cities because of the changing level of demand for their labor. Blacks who were once needed in great numbers to work the southern plantations became superfluous as mechanization came to the farms and orchards. At the same time, the new agricultural technologies required more capital than small farmers could muster, and much of the marginally economic cotton and tobacco land converted to cattle grazing and timber growing which required few workers.

The technological revolution in southern agriculture since World War II is often heralded as a marvel of economic development, but such analyses do not take into account that it was largely financed by federal funds which developed rural electrification, new machinery, advanced high-yield crops, concentrated fertilizers, and insecticides. In addition, while farmers received federal money *not* to produce crops through "soil bank" and other programs, the tens of thousands of workers thus displaced were not compensated or retrained (*Wall Street Journal* December 15, 1967; *Barron's Weekly* June, 1968:1). They drifted to the cities where, ill-trained and unused to urban ways, they enlarged welfare rolls in Cincinnati, Washington, D.C., Chicago, and innumerable other cities.

A Broken Blue-Collar Ladder. While the demand for emigration of Blacks from the South parallels the experience of many other groups, their experience in the industrial North has been quite different because of the changing demands of technology, both machine and social. Negroes have enjoyed expanded employment opportunities in each of America's twentieth century wars, but these periods only temporarily obscure the long-term trends toward lower employment opportunities for unskilled immigrants (Mueller 1969; Faunce 1968). While earlier immigrants readily found employment opportunities, recent Black immigrants have found fewer jobs which they were able to fill.

What is of equal importance for immigrants is that contemporary bottom-level jobs typically do not prepare the worker for more advanced employment. In most industries there is now no craft skill hierarchy through which motivated workers can rise. The basic steel industry affords a case in point. Sixty years ago it employed many immigrants in back-breaking, hot, and dangerous jobs around the hearth. As a man learned English and the workings of the industrial process he could move up to higher paying, less arduous, safer, and cleaner positions. Today, by contrast, most of the unskilled jobs have been eliminated by technological advances, and those jobs which do remain provide no training for operating complex automatic equipment (Ross and Hill 1967).

The requirement of formal schooling, either because of the demands inherent in machine technology, or because of the regulations imposed by social technology through corporation or union regulations, has greatly limited the upper mobility of Blacks. Even in those industries where a craft skilled hierarchy still exists, most notably in the building trades industry, Blacks have been systematically excluded by union-imposed racial discrimination. The paucity of unskilled jobs and the systematic exclusion of Blacks from many labor unions have led Willhelm and Powell (1964) to ask "Who needs the Negro?"

A White-Collar Ladder. While the Blacks' chances of blue-collar job mobility in production industries has been bleak, the situation is rather different when one turns to the service sector. Negroes have always been represented here as domestic servants, waiters, and sleeping car porters, but these were stigmatized Negro jobs with no potential for mobility. Since President Truman formally integrated the United States Armed Forces in 1948, jobs with potential mobility have opened up at all levels in government, in hospitals, and in other large white-collar bureaucracies such as the telephone company, notably in the last decade.

The rapid expansion of employment in the service industries, together with regulations for employment and advancement on the basis of qualification and tenure, without regard for race in most service industries, has greatly facilitated the employment of Blacks. The gains in government are impressive; in 1940 only 5% of government employees were black. Today, while the number of government workers has nearly trebled and Blacks comprise 11% of the total United States labor force, they comprise nearly 15% of all government workers.

Outside government much of the expansion in job opportunities for Blacks has been in clerical and elementary technical jobs, but these tasks are increasingly being taken over by computer-based electronic systems. For example, hospitals concerned about rapidly rising labor costs, are mechanizing the jobs of laboratory technicians as rapidly as possible. It is doubtful whether government and other service industries will expand rapidly enough over the next several decades to absorb enough Blacks so that the "immigrant model" of integration will work for a sizable segment of black migrants.

DOWN SO LONG IT LOOKS LIKE UP

In all of our cities a growing segment of the population is growing up in what Seligman (1968) calls "permanent poverty." Moynihan (1968) notes that in New York in 1968 more than half a million children received welfare benefits. To eliminate poverty two different strategies have developed. These follow the previously discussed lines of paternalism and fraternalism.

Paternalism. The strategy of paternalism is seen in welfare programs which give individuals money, services, or goods so long as need is proven. The welfare system of today grew out of successful efforts to Americanize earlier immigrants. Services were provided while the newcomer was finding his way in the city and was getting established in a job. But when unemployment is chronic and endemic, as it has become for many ghetto dwellers, such "temporary" welfare becomes perpetual. A far-flung welfare bureaucracy has grown to administer to the poor (Moynihan 1968), while landlords, ghetto store owners, and innumerable pushers, gamblers, and extortionists prey on the poor. Thus, the welfare administration and these landlords and store owners have inadvertently helped to develop and perpetuate a "culture of poverty" (Seligman 1968).

Fraternalism. If the paternalistic mode of accommodating Blacks has its moralistic and its corrupt elements, then the fraternalistic mode, like its parallel in the earlier phase of the Industrial Revolution, has both revolutionary and conservative elements (Leggett 1968). For over a century, outspoken Blacks have called for and worked to create indigenous black economic, political, social, and cultural institutions. These have included such men as Frederick Douglass, W.E.B. DuBois, Marcus Garvey, the Black Muslims, Malcolm X, and the Black Panthers. The attention of Whites has always been drawn to *extreme* political demands which have focused on self-determination in one form or another. Little attention has been given to their *conservative* social objectives. Both the Black Muslims and Black Panthers in this era stress to their members the importance of the family, frugality in all expenditures, hard work, abstinence from stimulants such as drugs, obedience to law, the primacy of education, and the human dignity through "Black Pride." This listing of virtues is nearly identical with the goals which any welfare department has for its dependents, and Gage (1970) has proposed only half in jest that city welfare agencies quietly subsidize these militant black organizations so that they can more effectively propagate middle-class virtues in the ghetto.

Contemporary fraternalism can be greatly aided, as its earlier counterpart was, through reform in the administration of law and government programs. Enforcement of equal employment opportunities has begun to open many more jobs to Blacks. On the consumption side, numerous laws and regulations are beginning to be enforced which reduce the exploitation of ghetto dwellers by land owners, store owners, and the like. Many leading law schools are for the first time offering courses (often by student demand) which deal with poverty law and consumer protection.

Another important government program congenial with the fraternalist model is a negative income tax, or as we will refer to it here, "income maintenance." There are numerous variations in specific proposals for income maintenance, but its underlying philosophy allows every family a total income above the poverty level. To achieve this, direct payments are made to supplement earned income. An income maintenance program differs from welfare in that participants do not have to prove need and do not receive payments which are earmarked for specific purposes; they are free to spend their income as they see fit. Certainly unwise expenditures will be made, but evidence from the large-scale experimental programs of income maintenance show that very little of the new income thus made available goes to frivolous expenditures. As in the case of the early Industrial Revolution, the short-term costs of fraternalism in money expended and sporadic disruptions are far outweighed by the long-term benefits of full citizenship which the strategy of paternalism does not seem able to achieve.

WHITE-COLLAR DISCONTENT: TWO INTERPRETATIONS

In the opening section of this chapter, we pointed to the technological conditions which make for objective alienation in the jobs of white-collar functionaries. While there are innumerable studies of blue-collar workers and ghetto Blacks, there are few empirical studies of white-collar functionaries, and few bear on the question at hand—the expression and channelling of alienation-generated discontent.

The numerous essays on the white-collar technocrat which have appeared over the last twenty years alloy in differing proportions two distinct diagnoses which were presented in neary pure form two decades ago. The first of these, *The Lonely Crowd* by David Riesman was published in 1950; the second, *White Collar* by C. Wright Mills was published a year later. Both focus on social technology, ideology, and social structure, but these classes of variables enter at different points in their explanatory schemes. They will be discussed separately, because they are based on different assumptions about how to explain white-collar discontent; Mills focuses on organizational, political, and economic questions, while Riesman focuses primarily on changes in culture and personality.

C. Wright Mills. Mills traces the emergence of massive industrial corporations, big government, and large-scale organizations generally. The consequences of these changes in social technology are traced in the demise of the "old" self-employed entrepreneurial middle class and the emergence of the "new" organization-employee white-collar middle class. He sees little alienation in the work of the old middle class shopkeepers, family farmers, craftsman and small manufacturers. Their society is viewed as having a strong family, practical education, self-regulating economy, active civic life focused on the local community, and participatory democracy. The ideology of the entrepreneurial middle class is expressed in the simple phrase which Mills quotes from the director of the 1850 federal census, "Let us alone." Although the view is now widely challenged by social historians, Mills asserts that "...the world of the small entrepreneurs was self-balancing" (1951:9).

This picture of idyllic tranquility is contrasted with the conflictful world of the organization man. In the work of the new middle class, Mills sees all of the conditions of objective alienation reviewed above. What is more his view of their social structure is derived from this perceived fact of alienation. In many ways his analysis of the social structural consequences of alienation is parallel to that discussed above for blue-collar workers. He notes, for example, a focus on rising levels of consumption, escapist leisure, and an orientation to security and guaranteed welfare, rather than entrepreneural freedom of opportunity.

Mills does not consider the family, but focuses on politics and ideology. He asserts that the white-collar worker who functions on the job as a narrow specialist views the political sphere as the proper domain of specialists other than himself. He becomes then a "political indifferent" in sharp contrast to his old middle-class counterpart who was continually engaged in community affairs. The white-collar classes are seen by Mills as inevitably forming the rear guard of other more articulate political interest groups in society, sometimes following labor, but more often following the lead of corporate interests with which they identify ideologically.

Mills ends his book by saying that the new middle class is primed to follow a strong leader who appeals to its discontent by evoking politically conservative imagery. Ironically, the same year *White Collar* was published, Senator Joseph McCarthy rose to political eminence by appealing to the sentiments of patriotic anticommunism. McCarthy drew much of his support from the white-collar classes by successfully channelling their discontent against the scapegoat of an internal communist menace. Such a protofascist allegiance is not the only political reaction that the white-collar functionary can make, as David Riesman suggests.

David Riesman. Riesman, like Mills, analysed changes in the American middle classes over the past century. But he focuses less on the alienating conditions of work in bureaucratic settings and more on changes in defining "the good life" and how this changed definition has implications for the diverse elements of social structure.

Riesman defines ideology in terms of "social character," that aspect of personality which is shared by a wide range of individuals in a given society. He identifies three sorts of generalized social character within his survey of history. The first, *tradition-direction* need not concern us here, because it is not prevalent in industrial societies. The second, *inner-direction* characterizes the ideology of the entrepreneurial middle class and permeated much of the rest of society in the latter half of the nineteenth century and the first few decades of this. Inner-direction is identified as an orientation to a set of absolute general standards of conduct which are implanted in an individual early in life through strict home and school environment. These standards impel the inner-directed individual to strive hard and eschew pleasure throughout his life.

Riesman sees another orientation emerging rapidly since World War II in the urban, industrial, organizational environment; he calls it *other-direction*. Other-direction is defined as a generalized orientation to seek direction from peers and the mass media. The goals of the other-directed individual shift with that guidance; only the orientation to the tastes of "significant others" is constant. In the home and progressive schools, other-direction is taught as the ability to understand, fit in, adjust, and lead through popularity and style rather than competition and performance. The emphasis on achievement is as great here as earlier, but the arena of achievement has changed from production-work to consumption-leisure and politics. In the process, the elements of social structure—family, religion, education, and politics—change radically.

Critics of Riesman assert that other-direction was a characteristic element of American society well before the emergence of large industrial and bureaucratic work organizations (Lipset 1961). Insofar as this is true, it brings into question the causal connection between the distinctive alienating conditions of contemporary white-collar jobs and the emergence of other-direction. Riesman might answer in defense of his view that the early forms of other-direction identified by Lipset were an important prerequisite for the rapid development of large-scale corporate organization in this century. Clearly this would not be the only example of an ideology emerging *before* the technology with which it becomes closely linked. Recall that in Chapter II we noted the importance of the Protestant Ethic in fostering the emergence of entrepreneurial production technologies.

Riesman, like Mills, sees white-collar work as alienating, and sees the prime adaptation as a flight into consumption; but Riesman, unlike Mills, does not view this process as simply a neurotic or pathological escape. He views it as basic to a normal and constructive adaptation to the emergence of a society of affluence.

Riesman's view of contemporary society informs our discussion in the next chapter. Suffice it here to compare Riesman's discussion of other-directed politics with that of Mills' reviewed above. Like Mills, Riesman sees the contemporary white-collar worker as indifferent to the interest group politics typical of an earlier era. The lonely crowd is thus susceptible to manipulation by the demagogue who can effectively use mass media. Unlike Mills, however, Riesman does not only point to this gloomy prospect for democracy; he sees the emergence of a vast diversity of new organized interest groups. Whereas old interest groups were based on relationships of production—business, finance, farming, laboring—each new interest group focuses on a much more narrow concern, but together they represent a fuller range of institutional areas of contemporary life. Such groups would include the National Education Association, Sierra Club, Planned Parenthood, National Rifle Association, Freedoms Fund, Friends Committee on National Legislation, Wool Institute, National Sharecroppers Fund, and Morality in the Media Fund. Through such organizations and innumerable others, Riesman argues, the work-alienated white-collar functionary is creatively drawn into the arena of civic and political life. Even when he is not an active member in such groups, his attitudes are shaped by them through the press and television.

With Riesman's view of contemporary political processes, this brief chapter on the individual and the crucible has come full circle. It began by tracing the alienating conditions inherent in many contemporary work situations, then pointed to some pathological accommodations to alienation, but with Riesman we see the suggestion that alienation in work may be requisite for the full participation of individuals in the society which is emerging.

Chapter 6

PLANNING AND SOCIOLOGY IN THE CRUCIBLE

The human species is genetically little changed from what it was two centuries ago at the outset of the Industrial Revolution; yet in that short span of time purposive planning, a new mechanism of species survival, has been perfected, if not consistently used. This final chapter examines several ideological blocks to the full use of planning in the crucible of industry and sociology's place, past, present, and future, in this arena.

Attitudes Toward Planning

As noted in the first chapter, Americans have long had an antipathy to the idea of planning. But this statement needs to be qualified for it is only partially true. In practice, planning has been fostered in some areas as much as it has been inhibited in others. The present section of the chapter examines several prevalent ideological stances toward planning with particular emphasis on the industrial realm. First, it explores the meaning of this much maligned term, "planning."

CUSTOM AND PLANNING

One of the defining characteristics of the process of industrialization is the widening arenas of social life in which planning replaces custom. As the traditional craft skill of the master has been replaced by the design engineer, just so the horsesense of the entrepreneur has been replaced by the economics of the business administrator, the conventional wisdom of the family doctor has been replaced by the technical prowess of a battery of medical specialists, and the cracker barrel politician has been replaced by the bureau administrator. Even the art of love-making is now explored dispassionately by scientists and merchandized in *Playboy* (Lewis and Brissett 1967).

Planning involves a scheme or procedure for attaining some goal. In this loose sense, planning is not unique to industrial society. As the word is used here the process involves the objective collection of information on alternative means of attaining a goal, and the choosing among alternatives in terms of rational criteria, such as convenience, cost, efficiency, or the like. Such planning on a routine basis *is* uniquely characteristic of industrial societies (Weber 1961:258-70; Mannheim 1941:140-96).

Planning involves at least three interdependent elements. First, there must be a dispassionate view of the phenomena under investigation. There must be a willingness to look beyond dogma, custom, convention, and vested interests of any sort. Second, a phenomenon must be viewed as part of a system of interrelated elements, operating in terms of known or partially known laws, such as the laws of nature, economics, or sociology. Finally, there must be methods for effectively intervening in the system. Opponents of planning are quite right in asserting that planning tends to demystify and expose venerable beliefs and assumptions. But our growing knowledge about the chemical components of the moon's surface and of love-making does not make the object or the process any less beautiful although it may influence the definition of beauty (Northrop 1949:291-311).

Each of the three elements listed above influences the others. Without a dispassionate view of a phenomenon there is not likely to be a search for effective means of intervention. So long as poverty was viewed as the product of personal incapacity and sloth in a land of unlimited opportunity, for example, there was no great effort to find means of eliminating it because poverty was defined as inevitable. What is more, there is strong resistance to planning in part because once the process is begun, widely held practices and beliefs may be called into question. To plan for the eradication of poverty begs the question "Who profits from poverty?"

Family Planning: An Example. For generations rational family planning met lively resistance on customary and religious grounds. In those times the only means of control were sexual abstinence, abortion, and infanticide. But this has changed with the introduction of effective contraceptive techniques in recent years. American women now consume over 42,000,000 contraceptive pills a day (Soderlind 1970:1) and the attitude toward family planning has changed rapidly. The emerging view that it is better for all concerned that no unwanted child be brought into the world is changing the public attitude toward abortion. This new view has fostered efforts to change laws to make abortion less costly in both financial and psychic terms (Udry 1971:391–423).

Modern techniques of contraception invalidate the age-old adage that "the woman pays" for pre- and extra-marital sexual relations. Contraception makes possible a radical alteration in the sexual mores of the young which is only just beginning to take place (Moskin 1969). Contraceptive techniques also place family planning in the hands of women, allowing them greater freedom to *plan* for activities in addition to marriage (Rossi 1968; Orden and Bradburn 1969), thus altering the imbalance of power between the sexes in Western society (Winick 1968). Rather than reduce the power of men, "women's liberation" holds the promise of making possible a richer relationship between the sexes which benefits both, because men no longer need to maintain an exaggerated posture of masculinity (Roszak and Roszak 1969; Skolnick and Skolnick 1971).

PLANNING, A DIRTY WORD

In their study of business and its environment, Davis and Bloodstrom (1966: Ch. 10) present several examples of businessmen who have used government research, tax exemption, loans, concessions, and other government aid to gain financial success while stridently decrying "government encroachment on free enterprise." In another study Berg (1963) shows how the business community blames the government for economic recession, while, it asserts that recovery can only be made by giving business a free hand.

These are contemporary expressions of laissez faire, an attitude toward planning which goes back two centuries to the followers of Adam Smith. In its simplified ideological form, it asserts that the entire society benefits when each individual business is allowed to plan (though this word is seldom used) for its own self-interests and when government planning and other "fetters" on free competition are eliminated (Monson 1963). Whatever correspondence to the day-to-day workings of the economy that the laissez faire ideology had in the early nineteenth century has been vitiated by the emergence of corporate capitalism in the past eighty years (Bain 1959; Galbraith 1967). Nonetheless, laissez faire ideology is still widely asserted. The idea has survived because it is useful for three related reasons. It provides the industrial businessman a basis for asserting that his success is due to his efforts alone, that he deserves a rich reward for his efforts, and his activity has been in the best interests of the country (Sutton, Harris, Kaysen, and Tobin 1956; Rischin 1965; Wyllie 1966).

It is used by large corporation spokesmen to maintain the legal and political fiction that their companies have no different place in society or impact on the economy than did the "ma and pa" drugstore or blacksmith shop of yesteryear (Monson 1963; Schonfeld 1965; Baran and Sweezy 1966). Beyond this, the laissez faire idea has been used to show how planning on the part of business is right and proper while planning by government is necessarily bad (Arnold 1937:118–35; Hempel 1939; Mills 1951: 35–62; Hamilton 1957:3–62; Randall 1961; Rischin 1965; Epstein 1969). The question of *who* should plan and for *what* ends is complex but to identify laissez faire as *ideology* is not necessarily to embrace the counter-ideology of the various critics of business; rather it is to show how the laissez faire ideology draws attention away from the possibility that families, government agencies, voluntary organizations, and others outside the business sphere may legitimately engage in planning activities. The business community is not alone in its antipathy to the idea of social planning, and in fact, a much more encompassing criticism comes from the humanistic critics of industrial society, a subject to which we now turn.

FEAR OF *La Technique*

In Chapter 1 we noted that "planning" is often equated with the monolithic totalitarian plans of Nazi Germany and Stalinist Russia. A number of other authors see planning as monolithic and repressive, not because of its imposition by a political party, but because it is a natural consequence of a technological determinism inherent in the process of industrialization itself. This idea is captured neatly in Adlai Stevenson's assertion that "technology, while adding daily to our physical ease, throws daily another loop of fine wire around our souls" (1955).

Jacques Ellul (1964) is a most eloquent exponent of this global indictment of planning. He bemoans the contemporary scene as a society of *means* in which man is alienated from all meaningful *goals*. In his view contemporary society is a product of the social technology of planning applied to every facet of human existence. This ever more pervasive planning he calls *"la technique"* and traces its application in work, sports, war, politics, leisure, and all other realms of modern life.

Ellul does not stand alone in this indictment of contemporary society earlier voiced by Ortega y Gasset in his *Revolt of the Masses*. He is joined by a number of European scholars reared in the backwash of World War I who reached maturity in the holocaust of World War II. Representative authors in this tradition and their works include F. G. Juenger, *The Failure of Technology,* Raymond Aron, *Progress and Dissolution: The Dialectic of Modern Society,* Herbert Marcuse, *One Dimensional Man,* and E. J. Mishan, *Technology and Growth,* and Erich Fromm, *Escape from Freedom.* Many of the pathologies they outline are real enough, but their pessimistic and facile generalizations of technological determinism foster a rather myopic view of man the machine maker damned by his own creations, and inhibit creative efforts to use new found tools of planning to *overcome* the pathological consequences of industrialization. Nevertheless, the fatalistic view of this school has profoundly influenced both social scientists and policy makers. Their prejudice against technology is illustrated in their view of the mass media. They note that Hitler and the Italian Fascists used the mass media to fulfill their propaganda purposes, and that in America the media deal exclusively in artless pap which is a kind of fantasy escape from the real world. From these observations they conclude that the new technologies necessarily suppress freedom of expression and help to create a sort of mass man (Adorno 1938; Gans 1966).

Leaving aside the prejudgments of the technological pessimists, it is apparent that television has a potential much greater than that of purveyor of propaganda and mind-dulling entertainment. Clearly, television has changed our perception of national and world events, has introduced new standards of consumption to the ghetto and to the middle classes, has influenced politics in diverse ways, has reconstituted preschool education, and has been a requisite element in fostering the civil rights movement, ghetto riots, and concerns with environment over the past decade (Lang and Lang 1968; Chester 1969; Mendelsohn and Crespi 1970). If Marshall McLuhan (1964) is right, television and the related electronic media are reshaping the very ways in which we think. One may be disturbed by or applaud these influences, but they were not foreseen by the technological pessimists. Put differently, the modern technologies may be used for propaganda, mind-dulling entertainment, selling mouthwash, or reconstituting political prophecies, but the choice is ours and is not inherent in the technology itself, as the technological pessimists would have us believe.

TECHNOCRATIC LAISSEZ FAIRE

Another group of writers on technology embrace the planning process as an end in itself. The only "problems" they discuss are those of implementation and further development. They express what we will call technocratic laissez faire ideology, which, while left implicit, assumes that the interests of the whole society are best advanced by each technical specialty pursuing its own perfection. This technocratic view was discussed in Chapter 5 and is reflected in most of the articles reprinted in *Engineering: Its Role in Society*, edited by Davenport and Rosenthal (1967) and in *Technology in American Life*, edited by Carroll W. Persell, Jr. (1969). A recent work in this technocratic tradition is *Information Technology and Organizational Change* by Thomas L. Whisler (1970).

In practice technocratic laissez faire planning for society has, for the most part, been focused on satisfying the needs of those organizations, groups, and interests which have been able to pay for technical expertise. Planning has thus tended to serve rather narrow interests in society. A most relevant case in point can be drawn from the business community's continuing interest in social reform. In an earlier era business was much interested in social planning. The Americanization programs of immigrants were largely financed by industry, as were the various welfare movements of the Salvation Army and Women's Christian Temperance Union. Business leaders helped to finance the various "antisaloon leagues" because they promised to deliver to the factory gate each Monday morning workers who were both sober and docile (Gusfield 1963). The role of business in championing social reform laws that would serve its interests during the decades around the turn of the century has been well documented by Chamberlain (1967), Fine (1969), Wiebe (1968) and Weinstein (1968).

While specific targets of reform may have changed since that time, there is no evidence that laissez faire planning today better serves society (Mishan 1970). Corporation executives and writers in business oriented magazines continually stress that it is in business' self-interest to maintain stability in society. They advocate programs to help improve jobs, housing, and education for the underprivileged. These efforts are usually short-lived because they threaten other vested interests such as white labor unions, slum landlords, or the city welfare bureaucracy. What is more, such programs may be attacked by corporation stockholders for they neither bring profit nor uniformly positive publicity to the corporation (Sethi 1970:123–38).

DEFENSIVE PLANNING

For over a generation an increasing proportion of corporation resources has gone into the research and development of new and improved products (Galbraith 1962; Schon 1967). And yet the planning activities of industrial firms are often used to *forestall* change, *stifle* technological innovation, and *reduce* market competition. This has been accomplished by organizational changes which collectively may be called "defensive planning." In industries which had been quite competitive this involved the development of oligopoly. Burlington Mills, for example, has recently come to the fore in textiles. It announced its emerging dominance through television commercials which boast, "If it has anything to do with textiles, Burlington does more of it and does it better than anyone else." Georgia Pacific has recently achieved a similar predominent position in the lumber and wood products industry.

General Motors, quite sensitive to the charge of dominating the domestic automobile market, has been content to hold approximately 45 percent of the market in its own name. At the same time it has contracted with its two prime "competitors," Ford and Chrysler, to build components for their automobiles! As early as 1964, 41 of General Motors' 130 plants produced Ford and Chrysler components (Raskin 1964: 68; *Wall Street Journal* November 24, 1970:30). How widespread this ingenious practice of manufacturing products for a competitor to evade antitrust action may be is unknown.

A decade ago it was thought that the presence of alternative products helped to maintain market competition and an incentive toward innovation even in industries dominated by oligopolies. Thus, it was reasoned, competition from aluminum and plastics would keep steel prices from getting too high and would motivate research efforts (Galbraith 1952; Schumpeter 1934:132–33). This view is now widely challenged (Elzinga 1968). What is more, the trend toward conglomerate mergers, discussed in Chapter 4, has complicated the issue (Kohlmeier 1969:28). The major steel companies are buying aluminum and chemical plastic companies (*Wall Street Journal* August 9, 1968:3). In like manner the major oil companies are buying into the coal industry, and auto companies are moving into rapid transit railroads and highway ventures (*Wall Street Journal* February 13, 1968).

The reasons for purchases in competing products are undoubtedly complex, but this activity in the oil-coal case is most telling. In recent years oil companies have bought coal companies in the wake of the announcement that a commercially feasible technique for extracting gasoline from low grade coal deposits has been perfected, and in fear of a national fuel shortage (*New Republic* April 9, 1966:7; *Barron's Weekly* July 8, 1968; *Wall Street Journal* March 8, 1968:2, 27). It is significant to note that the federal Department of the Interior spent $10 million in sponsoring the research, but the patents for the coal-to-gasoline conversion process are held by the Consolidated Coal Company. Here we have an example of one of the contemporary means of converting public funds into private profit.

This example illustrates another form of conglomerate self-protection. Continental Oil may have bought Consolidated Coal not to *use* the newly patented process but to insure that it will *not* be used by a competitor (*New Republic,* April 9, 1966:7; *Wall Street Journal* December 21, 1970:3). The same has been said of the recent interest of the large auto companies in the development of electric automobile engines: if the companies control the key patents on electrical engines, then they will be able to protect their huge investments in conventional gasoline engine production.

The Wankel Case. Such planning for self-protection is only speculation, but the successful efforts of the major automobile makers around the world to stop the introduction of the Wankel engine by controlling patent rights is documented. The Wankel engine is a combustion motor which has no pistons; it is smaller, lighter, more economical, and more easily repaired than a comparable conventional engine. Its introduction would mean a great loss to motor companies which have huge sunk costs in conventional engine production and repair facilities. A decade ago ,when the Wankel engine was perfected, some experts predicted that it would entirely replace conventional auto engines in the near future. But of course the history of its introduction has been quite different. It has been put in no American-built automobile and is only now on the market in an expensive obscure German sports sedan, the NSU, RO-80. The early Wankel engine emitted higher levels of pollution than comparable conventional engines, but this problem was of no great concern to auto developers until the late 1960s.

The reason for this slow deployment is not technological but organizational. The Wankel patents were purchased by the major automobile interests to keep the engine *off* the market and to make sure no rival introduces the engine (Schliewen 1970). A grand cartel of European automobile producers linking the two prime European mass market rivals Fiat and Volkswagen and including Citroen, BMW, Ferrari, Mercedes-Benz, and Peugot, recently has been formed to insure that all auto interests share in the decisions about when and how the Wankel engine will be introduced (*Der Spiegel* March 17, 1969); General Motors recently has joined this cartel (*Wall Street Journal* November 3, 1970:4; Camp 1971:1, 15).

In Defense of Defensive Planning. The term defensive planning is not meant as a negative evaluation of planning by corporations. In fact it would be surprising to find planning which is oriented to any other goal than self-defense, be they individuals, organizations, or biological organisms changing only insofar as they need to adapt to changing external circumstances. Seen in this perspective the most general policy question is how to shape the context in which defensive planning takes place so that it will serve the best interests of all. This is a tall order but in recent years a number of political scientists, economists, lawyers, and sociologists, have turned their attention to one or another aspect of this general problem. Rather than attempt to summarize or interpret this growing and diverse literature we now turn to a review of the role of sociology in the crucible of industry.

The Place of Sociology

As noted in Chapter 1, sociology was a product of the Industrial Revolution. Its focus is still primarily upon those aspects of society which are in turmoil because of the continuing industrial revolution and its various by-products. Yet sociology has not been able to cure society's ills so easily as its founding fathers such as Saint-Simon and Comte had promised. In part the past failures of sociology can be attributed to its immaturity of methods and theory. Part of the failure of sociology is due to its misinterpretation and misuse in the planning-policy realm. These problems will be focal in this concluding part of the chapter.

Sociology Misunderstood

In a recent review of the state of sociology, Neil Smelser and James Davis (1969:122–26) discuss five points of tension between sociologists and planners who would use their work. Each of these is relevant to the use of sociology in the crucible of industry. First, "Sociologists necessarily study and make public some things that many people would prefer to keep in the social closet, as it were" (p. 122). This problem is endemic in the competitive industrial sphere where information is an asset to be jealously guarded both between firms and within the firm. Thus, the needs of industrial secrecy often thwart the efforts of sociologists in industry to get information necessary for their planning-related research. Even the *sponsors* of industrial research may not disclose all of the information sociologists need for thorough research, resulting in research conclusions which may be poorly founded.

Using diverse examples of industrial, governmental, and espionage data collection, Wilensky (1967) has impressively shown that public techniques of intelligence gathering provide more accurate information than do those techniques which are clandestine. This is due, in a large part, Wilensky finds to the fact that while all information can be tailored to fit a desired planning strategy, secret information cannot be tested and checked by the normal canons of science. Wilensky concludes, "In the end, the most reliable intelligence sources of competing organizations are open; the best data, seldom secret, are the actions of the other party" (Wilensky 1967:72). He points to the Council of Economic Advisors as a model for the proper use of social scientists in a planning-policy arena. It uses public data, makes information available to all, and has developed no complex organizational structure which might distort information to serve its *own* needs as the CIA has done.

Second, planners often demand answers of sociologists even when they are not able to research questions completely. At the same time sociologists are not accepted as "experts" to the same degree that engineers and economists have been. Thus, to be heard within the corporation, sociologists may "oversell" the partial answers they do have and eventually be discredited in the eyes of planners when their proposals are not fully effective. A good example of this cycle is afforded by the "human relations" approach to industrial relations (discussed in Chapter 4), which some advisors claimed was a panacea for industry several decades ago. The expertise of sociologists is most likely to be challenged when their findings bring into question cherished beliefs or presumed fundamental "facts." Sociologists have made numerous proposals of ways to reduce the alienating conditions of factory work, for example, but most of these have been rejected as being threatening to "managerial prerogatives" or established engineering principles.

Third, the statements made by sociologists, like those of all scientists, are given in the form of probabilistic generalizations while their clients usually want predictions for a specific instance. Criminologists, for example, can give accurate statements on the rate of recidivism for the population of men released from prison, but parole officers want to know whether a particular prisoner is a good prospect for parole.

Fourth, planners usually ask for strategies which will *change* a given state of affairs while sociologists search for the *causes* of an event or condition. Knowledge of the major causes are not of interest to the planner because causal factors are most usually beyond the influence of planners. A demographer may accurately say that the reduction in birth rates is primarily determined by industrialization and concomitant changes in values, but a planner cannot wait for industrialization to incur. The demographer may also say that a densely populated and poor country cannot industrialize without first reducing its birth rate! What the planner needs in in this instance is information on how to implement a birth control plan, because while he cannot easily industrialize, he can set up birth control control clinics and the like. As Gouldner (1957) notes, this is the difference between the needs of the sociologist's "pure theory" and the planner's "applied theory." While pure theory, what Saint-Simon called "social physics," focuses attention on those variables which most completely explain the phenomena under study, applied theory, what might be called *social engineering,* focuses attention on those variables most accessible to deliberate manipulation.

SOCIOLOGY MISUSED

A fifth point of tension between sociology and the larger society mentioned by Smelser and Davis (1969) is based not so much on the misunderstanding as on the *misuse* of knowledge. They phrase this point quite fastidiously: "By and large the professional sociologist has a strong loyalty to the tradition of scientific and humanistic learning as institutionalized in centers of higher education. Those who seek his knowledge or counsel are almost always in some other kind of organizational setting (a business firm, for instance) and for that reason have loyalties to other types of values (the epic of profit-maximization, for instance). This circumstance tends to generate difficulties of communication and perhaps conflicts of values between the two. And a sociologist who takes employment in an organization other than a college or university may experience feelings that he has fallen in status or even 'sold out' " (p. 124). A number of sociological critics have cited particular sociologists or sociology in general for having "sold out" by becoming, in Baritz's (1960) term "servants of power" (Lynd 1939; Mills 1959; Stein and Vidich 1963; Horowitz 1968; Reynolds and Reynolds 1970; Beals, 1969; Friedrichs 1970; Gouldner 1968, 1970).

Loren Baritz (1960) has reviewed the various ways American industrial firms have employed social scientists. Citing the sorts of studies we have reviewed in Chapter 5 concerning workers, he concludes that social science research has been used by management primarily to find ways of inexpensively increasing productivity and to maintain the loyalty of blue-collar workers. As far as sociologists in industry are concerned, his indictment of exploitation is quite unfair.

Many sociologists did do research in factories in the decade following World War II, but as many of them "sided" with labor as with management, and most were not openly partisan. What is more important, there immediately developed in the professional journals a lively debate over the legitimate place of sociology in the industrial arena which sensitized all to the issues involved (Blumer 1947; Moore 1947; Gouldner 1948; Schneider 1950; Sorensen 1951; Stone 1952; Koivisto 1953; Wilensky 1957).

Those researchers who became apologists for the business interests were soon ignored by the sociological research community. Studies which were based more on some nostrum for improving industrial relations than on objective data were soon discredited, and valuable studies became as much a part of the union's as of the management's planning processes. Ironically, the human relations approach which was devised to adjust blue-collar workers to the assembly line is now used mostly to fit management personnel into a smooth working management team (Strauss 1968)! What is more, these servants of power are soon ignored by business too, because their schemes, created more to please their clients than to affect change, proved of little use in meeting the needs of management (Peterson 1962a).

The clients of research in industry most often have been management, and these management interests have shaped the research forms. As a result there has been more research focused on the "problems" which managers have with workers and white-collar functionaries than with "problems" which management causes workers or society. More recently the concern about the contribution of industry to the problems of pollution, to international unrest through the traffic in armaments (Peck and Scherer 1962; Thayer 1969; Kemp 1970), to the competition over internation oil rights (Engler 1966; O'Connor 1968; Tanzer 1969), and the like, have spawned much research. Nonetheless it is still true that most of this research is done by persons other than sociologists, by those not in the major universities, and by persons using styles of investigation more in the tradition of journalistic reporting than in that of scientific research.

For sociology to fully serve the interests of management—or any other client—it must be free to range beyond the technical questions posed by the client. The sociologist must explore the goals, structure, and dynamics of client organizations, because social problems usually cannot be solved in isolation. As Gouldner (1956) has shown, the problems defined by the client are most often symptoms of more basic ills.

THE SOCIOLOGICAL PERSPECTIVE

To this point we have focused on how information supplied by sociologists can be used in the planning process. As Smelser and Davis (1969) suggest, sociology can make another important contribution by helping to provide a more systematic way of thinking about societal planning. In the first critique of sociology written after World War II, C. Wright Mills (1959) argued that sociology should be vitally engaged in the planning process. He called this orientation the "sociological imagination" because it makes its possessor better able to see the link between the daily events of his life and the workings of society at large (Mills 1959:3–7).

We will use the term "perspective" rather than "imagination" because Mills incorporated two elements in his concept which we do not intend here. The sociological imagination leads him to see society as dominated by a few monolithic power groups, while we believe what will be seen is still moot. The sociological perspective is not a *particular* view of the social world but a means of formulating the proper questions and searching for alternative answers. In addition, Mills described it as a tool which an individual might use to *understand* his fate. We see it rather as an instrument which one can use in order to change his fate (Peterson 1962b).

The sociological perspective is a method of viewing a social world which is expressed in the "functionalist" or "system" theories of most sociologists. Society is seen as a system whose parts are loosely linked together in multiple ways. The loose and multiple linkages make for continuous conflict in the system. Such conflict in turn may make for system growth or decay.

This model directs the sociologist and the planner to look for the unintended as well as the intended consequences of any activity. It directs them to seek out the functions of each activity on the assumption that no activity, whether it be desired or not, would long survive if it did not fill some need. Finally, it directs researchers to look for alternative elements which might serve the same purpose at less cost to the system because this view assumes that no activity or element is uniquely required for system maintenance (Merton 1968; Berrien 1968; Demerath and Peterson 1967).

This perspective is distinctly sociological (rather than psychological, economic, or legalistic) because of the conceptual level of categories, variables, and propositions employed. Explanations for human behavior are sought in the group-allegiances people hold and in the social categories with which they can be identified. In this view society is seen as a more or less integrated set of social institutions which together comprise what we earlier defined as social structure. Finally, individual and institutional behavior is seen as set in a matrix of poorly articulated beliefs, values, norms, and ideologies, which are changing over time, and determining the limits within which individual and organizational activity takes place. This perspective on society is exemplified by the authors cited at the end of the first part of this chapter. We believe with many others that the sociological perspective is a strategically important tool, because the manifold problems of contemporary life come not so much from our technological incapacity as from our limited and faltering control over the processes of society.

All this said, it is now possible to see that the purpose of this short work has been by assertion and example to sharpen the reader's sociological eye by focusing on some of the social problems created by the continuing industrial revolution. The book's goal has been reached if the reader can now see better much of what has *not* been discussed here.

SELECTED REFERENCES

ABRAHAMSON, MARK (ed.)
1967 *The Professional in the Organization.* Chicago: Rand McNally.

ADORNO, T. W.
1938 "Uber den fetischcharakter in der Musik." *Zeitschrift fur Sozialforschung* 7:321–56.

AIKEN, MICHAEL and JERALD HAGE
1966 "Organizational alienation: A comparative analysis." *American Sociological Review* 31:497–507.

AIKEN, MICHAEL, LOUIS A. FERMAN, and HAROLD L. SHEPPARD
1968 *Economic Failure, Alienation, and Extremism.* Ann Arbor: University of Michigan Press.

ANDERSON, DAVID C.
1968 "Muted whistle-stops: Escalated termination of passenger trains causes woes for hundreds of communities." *Wall Street Journal* (February 13): 1, 9.

ARNOLD, TRUMAN
1937 *The Folklore of Capitalism.* New Haven, Conn.: Yale University Press.

AUERBACH, CARL, LLOYD K. GARRISON, WILLARD HURST, and SAMUEL MERMIN.
1961 *The Legal Process.* Scranton, Pa.: Chandler.

BACKES, CLARUS
1969 "The cabbies: A front-seat view." *Chicago Tribune* (February 23) :D21–31.

BAIN, JOE S.
1959 *Industrial Organization.* New York: John Wiley.

BAKER, FRANK, PETER J.M. MCEWEN, and ALAN SHELDON (eds.)
1969 *Industrial Organizations and Health: Selected Readings.* London: Tavistock.

BANFIELD, EDWARD C.
1958 *The Moral Basis of a Backward Society.* New York: Free Press.

BARAN, PAUL A. and PAUL M. SWEEZY
1966 *Monopoly Capital: An Essay on the American Economic and Social Order.* New York: Modern Reader.

BARITZ, LOREN
1960 *The Servants of Power: A History of the Use of Social Science in American Industry.* Middletown, Conn.: Wesleyan University Press.

Barron's National Business and Financial Weekly
1968 "Orville's green thumb: Farm policies have grown costlier and more wasteful than ever." (June 17) :1.

_____
1968 "The business front: Fuel of the future: Long-range prospects for coal have never looked brighter." (July 8) :11, 19.

_____
1968 "Dirty pooling: How to succeed in business without really trying." (July 15) :1, 9, 10, 12, 16, 18.

_____
1968 "Grapes of wrath: Freedom to buy and sell is perishable too." (August 5) :1.

BAUER, RAYMOND A., ITHIEL DE SOLA POOL, and LEWIS A. DEXTER
1963 *American Business and Public Policy.* New York: Atherton.

BEALS, RALPH L.
1969 *Politics of Social Research: An Inquiry into the Ethics and Responsibilities of Social Scientists.* Chicago: Aldine.

BECKER, HOWARD S.
1963 *Outsiders.* New York: Free Press.

BECKER, SELWYN W. and GERALD GORDON
1966 "An entrepreneurial theory of formal organizations, Part I: Patterns of formal organizations." *Administrative Science Quarterly* 11:315–44.

BEHREND, HILDE
1959   "Financial incentives as an expression of a system of beliefs."
        British Journal of Sociology 10 (June):256–64.
BELL, DANIEL
1959   "The racket-ridden longshoremen." Dissent 6 (Autumn):417–
        29.

――――
1960   The End of Ideology. New York: Free Press.
BELSHAW, CYRIL S.
1965   Traditional Exchange and Modern Markets. Englewood Cliffs,
        N.J.: Prentice-Hall.
BELZ, CARL
1969   The Story of Rock. New York: Oxford University Press.
BENDIX, REINHARD
1956   Work and Authority in Industry. New York: John Wiley.

――――
1959   "Industrialization, ideologies, and social structure." American
        Sociological Review 23 (September):613–23.

――――
1961   "The lower classes and the 'democratic revolution.' " Industrial
        Relations (October):1–34.
―――― and LLOYD H. FISHER
1949   "The perspectives of Elton Mayo." Review of Economics and
        Statistics 31:312–19.
BENNIS, WARREN G. and PHILIP E. SLATER
1968   The Temporary Society. New York: Harper & Row.
BENSMAN, JOSEPH
1967   Dollars and Sense: Ideology, Ethics, and the Meaning of Work
        in Profit and Nonprofit Organizations. New York: Macmillan.
―――― and ISRAEL GERVER
1963   "Crime and punishment in the factory: The functions of devi-
        ancy in maintaining the social system." American Sociological
        Review 28 (August):588–98.
BERG, IVAR
1963   "The confidence game." Columbia University Forum 6 (Win-
        ter):34–40.
BERLE, A. A. and G. C. MEANS
1932   The Modern Corporation and Private Property. New York:
        Macmillan.
BERNSTEIN, IRVING
1966   The Lean Years. Baltimore: Penguin.

BERRIEN, F. KENNETH
  1968   General and Social Systems. New Brunswick, N.J.: Rutgers
         University Press.

BERTON, LEE
  1969   "Companies that have merger bids rejected profit on stock
         sales." Wall Street Journal (January 27): 1, 14.

BJORK, GORDON C.
  1969   Private Enterprise and Public Interest. Englewood Cliffs, N.J.:
         Prentice-Hall.

BLAU, PETER M.
  1955   The Dynamics of Bureaucracy. Chicago: University of Chi-
         cago Press.

────── and OTIS DUDLEY DUNCAN
  1967   The American Occupational Structure. New York: John Wiley.

BLAUG, M. (ed.)
  1969   Economics of Education: Two. Middlesex, England: Penguin
         Books.

BLAUNER, ROBERT
  1960   "Work satisfaction and industrial trends in modern society,"
         in Walter Galenson and S.M. Lipset (eds.), Labor and Trade
         Unionism, pp. 339–60. New York: John Wiley.

──────
  1964   Alienation and Freedom: The Factory Worker and His Indus-
         try. Chicago: University of Chicago Press.

BLUM, FRED H.
  1953   Toward a Democratic Work Process. New York: Harper &
         Row.

BLUMER, HERBERT
  1947   "Sociological theory and industrial relations." American Socio-
         logical Review 12 (June):271–78.

──────
  1960   "Early industrialization and the laboring class." Sociological
         Quarterly 1 (January):16–32.

BLUNDELL, WILLIAM E.
  1968   "Los Angeles 'ghetto conglomerate' said to mark a new tack
         in war on poverty." Wall Street Journal (November 13):1, 19.

BOGUSLAW, ROBERT
  1965   The New Utopians. Englewood Cliffs, N.J.: Prentice-Hall.

BONJEAN, CHARLES M. and MICHAEL D. GRIMES
  1970   "Bureaucracy and alienation: A dimensional approach." Social
         Forces 48 (March):365–73.

BOWDICH, JOHN and CLEMENT RAMSLAND
1961   *Voices of the Industrial Revolution.* Ann Arbor: University of Michigan Press.

BOYER, RICHARD O. and HERBERT M. MORAIS
1955   *Labor's Untold Story.* New York: Cameron.

BRADBY, WESLEY
1969   "Social aspects of Argentine economic development." Nashville, Tenn.: unpublished manuscript.

BREZINSKI, ZBIGNIEW
1967   "The American transition." *New Republic* (December 23): 18–21.

BRODY, DAVID
1964   *Labor In Crisis: The Steel Strike of 1919.* Philadelphia: Lippincott.

BROWN, TERRY
1971   "Many small truckers go out of business." *Wall Street Journal* (February 24):24.

BROZEN, YALE
1963   *Automation: The Impact of Technological Change.* Washingington, D.C.: American Enterprise Institute for Public Policy Research.

BUDER, STANLEY
1968   *Pullman.* New York: Oxford University Press.

BUNTING, JOHN R.
1964   *The Hidden Face of Free Enterprise: The Strange Economics of the American Business Man.* New York: McGraw-Hill.

BURKE, JOHN G. (ed.)
1966   *The New Technology and Human Values.* Belmont, Calif., Wadsworth.

Business Week
1967   "He makes music pay at CBS." (October 7) 32:107–15.

──────
1970   "Capitol industries is off on another spin." (April 25):146–47.

CAMP, CHARLES B.
1971   "A scientist comes up with a 'perfect car'; Detroit just yawns." *Wall Street Journal* (March 15):1, 15.

CAREY, ALEX
1967   "The Hawthorne studies: A radical criticism." *American Sociological Review* 32 (June):403–16.

CAREY, JAMES T.
1969 "Changing patterns in the popular song." *American Journal of Sociology* 74:720–31.

CARLSON, ELLIOT
1968 " 'Soul food' catches on as black revolution spreads to the kitchen, chitterlings, black-eyed peas win fans in the North, negro restaurants' business booms." *Wall Street Journal* (November 27) :1.

CHAMBERLAIN, JOHN
1967 *Farewell to Reform: The Rise, Life and Decay of the Progressive Mind in America.* Chicago: Quadrangle Press.

CHANDLER, MARGARET K.
1964 *Management Rights and Union Interests.* New York: McGraw-Hill.

CHESTER, EDWARD W.
1969 *Radio, Television and American Politics.* New York: Sheed and Ward.

CHILD, JOHN
1969 *The Business Enterprise in Modern Society.* London: Crowell Collier and Macmillan.

CHINOY, ELI
1955 *Automobile Workers and the American Dream.* Garden City, N.Y.: Doubleday.

CLAY, JIM
1965 *Hoffa...Ten Angels Swearing.* Beaverdam, Va.: Beaverdam Books.

COCHRAN, THOMAS C.
1957 *The American Business System.* Cambridge, Mass.: Harvard University Press.

——— and WILLIAM MILLER
1961 *The Age of Enterprise.* New York: Harper & Row.

COLE, G. D. H. and RAYMOND POSTGATE
1961 *The British Common People.* New York: Barnes & Noble.

COLEMAN, JAMES S.
1970 "Social inventions." *Social Forces* 49 (December) : 163–73.

COLLINS, NORMAN R. and LEE E. PRESTON
1968 *Concentration and Price-Cost Margins in Manufacturing Industries.* Los Angeles: University of California Press.

COMMONS, JOHN R.
1918 *History of Labour in the United States.* Vol. I New York: Macmillan.

_____
1951 *The Economics of Collective Action.* New York: Macmillan.
CONNOR, MICHAEL J.
1970 "Program to establish negro auto agencies is running into trouble." *Wall Street Journal* (September 8):1, 10.
COTTRELL, W. F.
1951 "Death by dieselization: A case study in the reaction to technological change." *American Sociological Review* 16 (June): 358–65.
CRESSEY, DONALD R.
1969 *Theft of the Nation.* New York: Harper & Row.
CROZIER, MICHEL
1964 *The Bureaucratic Phenomenon.* Chicago: University of Chicago Press.
CURTIN, EDWARD R.
1965 "An evaluation of the impact of unions on wage differentials." *ILR Research* 11 (November):7–12.
DALTON, GEORGE (ed.)
1967 *Tribal and Peasant Economies.* Garden City, N.Y.: Natural History Press.
DANIELS, ROGER and HARRY H. KITANO
1970 *American Racism.* Englewood Cliffs, N.J.: Prentice-Hall.
DAVENPORT, WILLIAM H. and DANIEL ROSENTHAL (eds.)
1967 *Engineering: Its Role in Society.* Elmsford, N.Y.: Pergamon Press.
DAVIS, ALLISON
1946 "The motivation of the underpriviledged worker," in William F. Whyte (ed.), *Industry and Society.* New York: McGraw-Hill.
DAVIS, KEITH and ROBERT BLOODSTROM
1966 *Business and Its Environment.* New York: McGraw-Hill.
DAVIS, STANLEY M.
1968 "Entrepreneurial succession." *Administrative Science Quarterly* 13:402–16.
DECHERT, CHARLES R.
1968 *The Social Impact of Cybernetics.* New York: Simon & Schuster.

DEMERATH, N. J., III and RICHARD A. PETERSON (eds.)
  1967 *System, Change and Conflict.* New York: Free Press.

DENISOFF, R. SERGE and RICHARD A. PETERSON (eds.)
  1972 *The Sounds of Social Change: The Uses of Music in Contemporary Society.* Chicago: Rand McNally.

DENTLER, ROBERT A.
  1967 *Major American Social Problems.* Chicago: Rand McNally.

DIAMOND, SIGMUND
  1966 *The Reputation of the American Businessman.* New York: Harper & Row.

DIRLAM, JOEL B. and ALFRED E. KAHN
  1954 *Fair Competition.* Ithaca, N.Y.: Cornell University Press.

DUNLOP, JOHN T.
  1962 *Automation and Technological Change.* Englewood Cliffs, N.J.: Prentice-Hall.

DURKHEIM, EMILE
  1958 *Socialism and Saint-Simon.* Yellow Springs, Ohio: Antioch Press.

EGGERT, GERALD G.
  1967 *Railroad Labor Disputes: The Beginnings of Federal Strike Policy.* Ann Arbor: University of Michigan Press.

EISENSTADT, S. N.
  1964 "Breakdown of modernization." *Economic Development and Culture Change* 12 (July):345–67.

———
  1966 *Modernization: Protest and Change.* Englewood Cliffs, N.J.: Prentice-Hall.

ELIFSON, KIRK WHITE
  1968 "Job satisfaction of taxicab drivers." Nashville, Tenn.: Vanderbilt University, Master's thesis.

ELLUL, JACQUES
  1964 *The Technological Society.* New York: Knopf.

ELZINGA, KENNETH
  1968 "Oligopoly, the Sherman act and the new industrial state." *Social Science Quarterly* 49 (June):49–57.

EMERY, F. E. and E. L. TRIST
  1965 "The causal texture of organizational environments." *Human Relations* 18:21–31.

ENGLER, ROBERT
  1966 *The Politics of Oil.* Chicago: University of Chicago Press.

EPSTEIN, EDWIN M.
1969 *The Corporation in American Politics.* Englewood Cliffs, N.J.: Prentice-Hall.

ERASMUS, CHARLES J.
1961 *Man Takes Control: Cultural Development and American Aid.* Indianapolis: Bobbs-Merrill.

ETZIONI, AMITAI
1968a *The Active Society.* New York: Free Press.

———
1968b "Basic human needs, alienation and inauthenticity." *American Sociological Review* 33 (December):870–85.

——— (ed.)
1969 *The Semi-Professions and Their Organization.* New York: Free Press.

EVAN, WILLIAM M.
1962 "Due process of law in military and industrial organizations." *Administrative Science Quarterly* 7 (September):187–207.

FALCONE, NICHOLAS S.
1962 *Labor Law.* New York: John Wiley.

FAUNCE, WILLIAM A.
1965 "Automation and the division of labor." *Social Problems* 13 (Fall):149–60.

———
1968 *Problems of an Industrial Society.* New York: McGraw-Hill.

———, EINAR HARDIN, and EUGENE H. JACOBSON
1962 "Automation and the employee." *Annals of the American Academy of Political and Social Science* 340 (March):60–68.

FELDMAN, ARNOLD S. and WILBERT E. MOORE
1961 "Are industrial societies becoming alike?" St. Louis: paper presented at the American Sociological Association meetings (August).

FENSHAM, PETER J. and DOUGLAS HOOPER
1964 *The Dynamics of a Changing Technology.* New York: Humanities Press.

FERKISS, VICTOR C.
1970 *Technological Man.* New York: Mentor.

FILLOL, TOMAS ROBERTO
1967 *Social Factors in Economic Development: The Argentine Case.* Cambridge, Mass.: M.I.T. Press.

FINE, SIDNEY
1969 *Laissez Faire and the General-Welfare State: A Study of Conflict in American Thought 1865–1901.* Ann Arbor: University of Michigan Press.

FOOTE, NELSON N.
1953 "The professionalization of labor in Detroit." *American Journal of Sociology* 53 (January):371–80.

FORM, WILLIAM H.
1969 "Occupational and social integration of automobile workers in four countries: A comparative study." *International Journal of Comparative Sociology* 10 (March):95–116.

———— and DELBERT C. MILLER
1960 *Industry, Labor, and Community.* New York: Harper & Row.

FORRESTER, J. W.
1968 *Industrial Dynamics.* Cambridge, Mass.: M.I.T. Press.

FRAZIER, FRANKLIN E.
1957 *Black Bourgeoise: The Rise of a New Middle Class.* New York: Free Press.

FREUDENBERGER, H. and F. REDLICH
1964 "The industrial development of Europe: Reality, symbols, images." *Kyklos* XVII:372–403.

FRIEDMANN, GEORGES
1955 *Industrial Society: The Emergence of the Human Problems of Automation.* New York: Free Press.

FRIEDRICHS, ROBERT W.
1970 *A Sociology of Sociology.* New York: Free Press.

FROMM, ERICH
1941 *Escape from Freedom.* New York: Holt, Rinehart & Winston.

FULLAN, MICHAEL
1970 "Industrial technology and worker integration in the organization." *American Sociological Review* 35 (December):1028–39.

GAGE, RUTH C.
1970 "Black militants as agents of middle class reform." Nashville, Tenn.: unpublished manuscript.

GALBRAITH, JOHN KENNETH
1952 *American Capitalism.* Boston: Houghton Mifflin.

————
1962 *American Capitalism: The Concept of Countervailing Power.* Boston: Houghton Mifflin.

GALBRAITH, JOHN KENNETH
1967   *The New Industrial State.* Boston: Houghton Mifflin.

GANNON, JAMES
1968   "Labor organizations show mounting interest in combining forces." *Wall Street Journal* (March 7):1, 8.

GANS, HERBERT J.
1964   "The rise of the problem film." *Social Problems* 11:326–36.

――――
1966   "Popular culture in America: Social problem in mass society or social asset in a pluralist society," in Howard Becker (ed.), *Social Problems.* New York: John Wiley.

GINSBERG, ELI (ed.)
1964   *The Negro Challenge to the Business Community.* New York: McGraw-Hill.

GLASER, BARNEY G.
1964   *Organizational Scientists.* Indianapolis: Bobbs-Merill.

―――― (ed.)
1968   *Organizational Careers.* Chicago: Aldine.

GLAZER, NATHAN and DANIEL P. MOYNIHAN
1970   *Beyond the Melting Pot* (2nd ed.). Cambridge, Mass.: M.I.T. Press.

GOODE, WILLIAM
1961   "The librarian: From occupation to profession?" *Library Quarterly* 31 (October):306–18.

GOLDNER, FRED H.
1970   "The division of labor: Process and power," in Mayer N. Zald (ed.), *Power in Organizations.* Nashville, Tenn.: Vanderbilt University Press.

―――― and R. R. RITTI
1967   "Professionalization as career immobility." *American Journal of Sociology* (March):490–502.

GOLDSCHMIDT, WALTER R.
1947   *As You Sow.* New York: Harcourt Brace Jovanovich.

GORDON, ROBERT AARON
1961   *Business Leadership in the Large Corporation.* Berkeley: University of California Press.

GOULDNER, ALVIN W.
1948   "Discussion of the status and prospects of industrial sociology." *American Sociological Review* 13 (August):396:400.

――――
1952   "Red tape as a social problem," in Robert K. Merton, Alisa P.

Gray, Barbara Hockey, and Hanan C. Selvin, (eds.), *Reader in Bureaucracy*. New York: Free Press.

1954 *Wildcat Strike*. Yellow Springs, Ohio: Antioch Press.

1956 "Explorations in applied social science." *Social Problems* 3 (January):169–81.

1957 "Theoretical requirements of the applied social sciences." *American Sociological Review* 22 (February):92–102.

1968 "The sociologist as partisan: Sociology and the welfare state." *American Sociologist* 3 (May):103–16.

1970 *The Coming Crisis of Western Sociology*. New York: Basic Books.

————and Richard A. Peterson
1962 *Technology and the Moral Order*. Indianapolis: Bobbs-Merrill.

Graham, Ellen
1970 "Detergent industry, assailed for pollution, seeks new ingredients." *Wall Street Journal* (December 9):1.

Graves, Bennie
1970 "Particularism, exchange and organizational efficiency: A case study of a construction industry." *Social Forces* 49 (September):72–81.

Gregory, Charles O.
1961 *Labor and the Law*. New York: Norton.

Grob, Gerald N.
1969 *Workers and Utopia: A Study of Ideological Conflict in the American Labor Movement*. Chicago: Quadrangle.

Gusfield, Joseph R.
1963 *Symbolic Crusade*. Urbana.: University of Illinois Press.

Hacker, Andrew (ed.)
1965 *The Corporation Take-over*. Garden City, N.Y.: Doubleday (Anchor Books).

Haddad, William F. and G. Douglas Pugh (eds.)
1969 *Black Economic Development*. Englewood Cliffs, N.J.: Prentice-Hall.

Hall, Richard H.
1968 "Professionalization and bureaucratization." *American Sociological Review* 33 (February):92–104.

HALL, RICHARD H.
1969   *Occupations and Social Structure.* Englewood Cliffs, N.J.:
       Prentice-Hall.
HAMILTON, WALTON
1957   *The Politics of Industry.* Ann Arbor: University of Michigan
       Press.
HANSEN, NILES M.
1966   "Saint-Simon's industrial society in modern perspective."
       Southwestern Social Science Quarterly (December) :253–62.
HARVEY, EDWARD
1968   "Technology and the structure of organizations." *American
       Sociological Review* 33 (April):247–59.
HARWOOD, BOB
1971   "Factory housing faces more sticky obstacles than its boosters
       see." *Wall Street Journal* (April 8) :1, 17.
HEALY, S. J., CLETUS
1969   "Why the workers reject Chavez." *Twin Circle* (October 19):
       3–5.
HEILBRONER, ROBERT L.
1962   "The impact of technology: The historic debate," in John T.
       Dunlop (ed.), *Automation and Technological Change.* Engle-
       wood Cliffs, N.J.: Prentice-Hall.

———
1967   "Do machines make history?" *Technology and Culture* 8
       (July) :335–45.
HELLERSTEIN, JEROME R.
1963   *Taxes, Loopholes and Morals.* New York: McGraw-Hill.
HEMPEL, EDWARD H.
1939   *Industrial Political Economy.* New York: Pitman.
HENDERSON, W. O.
1969   *The Industrial Revolution in Europe.* Chicago: Quadrangle.
HENNINGER, DANIEL
1970   "And now lettuce." *New Republic* 163 (October 10) :9–11.
HERZBERG, FREDERICK, BERNARD MAUSNER, and BARBARA B. SNYDERMAN
1959   *The Motivation to Work.* New York: John Wiley.
HIRSCH, PAUL.
1969   *The Structure of the Popular Music Industry.* Ann Arbor:
       University of Michigan, Survey Research Center.
HOBSBAUM, E. J.
1959   *Primitive Rebels: Studies in Archaic Forms of Social Move-
       ment in the 19th and 20th Centuries.* New York: Norton.

HODGE, ROBERT W., PAUL M. SIEGEL, and PETER H. ROSSI
1964 "Occupational prestige in the United States, 1925–1963." *American Journal of Sociology* 70 (November):286–302.

HOLLES, EVERETT R.
1971 "American made...in Mexico." *New York Times* (January 31):1, 14.

HOROWITZ, IRVING L.
1968 *Professing Sociology*. Chicago: Aldine.

HOSELITZ, BERT F.
1964 "Karl Marx on secular economic and social development." *Comparative Studies in Society and History* 6 (January):142–63.

HOWTON, F. WILLIAM
1969 *Functionaries*. Chicago: Quadrangle.

HUIZINGA, JOHAN
1954 *The Waning of the Middle Ages*. New York: Doubleday.

HYATT, JIM
1969 "Service station men say big oil companies keep them in bondage." *Wall Street Journal* (October 7):1, 8.

INKELES, ALEX
1960 "Industrial man: The relation of status to experience, perception, and value." *American Journal of Sociology* 66 (July):1–31.

JACOB, HERBERT
1963 *German Administration Since Bismarck*. New Haven, Conn.: Yale University Press.

JAMES, RALPH C. and ESTELLE JAMES
1965 *Hoffa and the Teamsters: A Study of Union Power*. Princeton, N.J.: Van Nostrand Reinhold.

JAMES, RICHARD D.
1969 "Tired, young workers spur a steady increase in industrial accidents." *Wall Street Journal* (August 5):1, 18.

JANSSEN, RICHARD F.
1968 "New factory-bond rules are said to pose potential problems to firms, communities." *Wall Street Journal* (October 30):10.

KAHN, HERMAN and ANTHONY J. WIENER
1967 *The Year 2000*. New York: Macmillan.

KATZ, DANIEL and ROBERT L. KAHN
1966 *The Social Psychology of Organizations*. New York: John Wiley.

KAVOLIS, VYTAUTAS
1969 *Comparative Perspectives on Social Problems.* Boston: Little,
      Brown.
KAYSEN, CARL and DONALD F. TURNER
1959 *Antitrust Policy.* Cambridge, Mass.: Harvard University Press.
KEMP, GEOFFREY
1970 *Arms Traffic and Third World Conflicts.* New York: Carnegie
      Endowment for Peace (March).
KENNEDY, ROBERT F.
1960 *The Enemy Within.* New York: Popular Library.
KERR, CLARK, JOHN T. DUNLOP, FREDERICH HARBISON, and CHARLES A.
MYERS
1960 *Industrialism and Industrial Man.* New York: Oxford Uni-
      versity Press.
KERR, K. A.
1968 *American Railroads Politics, 1914–1920: Rates, Wages, and
      Efficiency.* Pittsburgh: University of Pittsburgh Press.
KLEIN, FREDERICH C.
1971 "Putting a new product on the market is costly, complicated—
      and risky." *Wall Street Journal* (February 18):1, 10.
KNOX, JOHN B.
1955 *The Sociology of Industrial Relations.* New York: Random
      House.
KOHLMEIER, LOUIS M.
1969 "FTC study hits growing closeness among biggest concerns,
      industries." *Wall Street Journal* (November 5):28.
———
1970 "High court's refusal to review injunction may bolster U.S.
      anticonglomerate drive." *Wall Street Journal* (January 13):
      4.
KOIVISTO, W.
1953 "Value, theory, and fact in industrial sociology." *American
      Journal of Sociology* 58 (May):564–72.
KOLKO, GABRIEL
1962 *Wealth and Power in America.* New York: Praeger.
KOMAROVSKY, MIRRA
1940 *The Unemployed Man and His Family.* New York: Dryden
      Press.
KORNHAUSER, ARTHUR
1964 *Mental Health of the Industrial Worker.* New York: John
      Wiley.

KORNHAUSER, WILLIAM
1962 *Scientists in Industry*. Berkeley: University of California Press.

KOVACK, BILL
1965 "The air-conditioned sweatshop." *Reporter* (October 7): 29–31.

KRAMER, JACK and DANFORTH W. AUSTIN
1971 "How a 1969 Mustang with a faulty one dollar part brings high estimates." *Wall Street Journal* (April 20):1, 10.

KUCZYNSKI, JURGEN
1967 *The Rise of the Working Class*. New York: McGraw-Hill.

LAING, JONATHAN R.
1970 "Daddy-O's attack on outlaw blacks." *Wall Street Journal* (November 23):16.

LANDES, DAVID S.
1969 *The Unbound Prometheus: Technological Change and Industrial Development in Western Europe from 1750 to the Present*. Cambridge, Mass.: Harvard University Press.

LANE, FREDERICK C.
1964 "Investment and usury in medieval Venice." *Explorations in Entrepreneurial History* 2 (Fall):3–15.

LANG, KURT and GLADYS ENGEL LANG
1968 *Politics and Television*. Chicago: Quadrangle.

LEGGETT, JOHN C.
1968 *Class, Race and Labor*. New York: Oxford University Press.

LENSKI, GERHARD E.
1966 *Power and Privilege*. New York: McGraw-Hill.

LEONARD, WILLIAM N. and MARVIN GLENN WEBER
1970 "Automakers and dealers: A study of criminogenic market forces." *Law and Society Review* 4 (February):407–24.

LESSING, LAWRENCE
1969 "The printed word goes electronic." *Fortune* 80 (September): 116–19.

LEVER, JANET
1969 "Soccer: Opium of the Brazilian people." *Trans-Action* 7 (December):36–43.

LEWIS, H. GREGG
1966 *Unionism and Relative Wages in the United States: An Empirical Inquiry*. Chicago: University of Chicago Press.

LEWIS, LIONEL and DENNIS BRISSETT
1967 "Sex as work: A study of avocational counseling." *Social Problems* 15 (January):8–17.

LINDSEY, ALMONT
1943   *The Pullman Strike.* Chicago: University of Chicago Press.

LIPSET, SEYMOUR MARTIN
1960   *Political Man.* Garden City, N.Y.: Doubleday.

———, and LEO LOWENTHAL (eds.)
1961   "A changing American character?" *Culture and Social Character.* New York: Free Press.

———, and EARL RAAB
1969   "The Wallace whitelash." *Trans-Action* 7 (December): 23–35.

———, MARTIN TROW, and JAMES COLEMAN
1956   *Union Democracy.* New York: Free Press.

LOEHWING, DAVID A.
1968   "Graphic advance: Makers of printing equipment are updating an age-old process." *Barron's Weekly* (July 29):3, 10–17.

LONDON, JOAN and HENRY ANDERSON
1970   *So Shall Ye Reap.* New York: Crowell Collier and Macmillan.

LONG, KENNETH
1968a "Edsel: Behind or ahead of its time?" Madison, Wisc.: unpublished manuscript.

———
1968b "A comparison of the social technology of trucking and carpentry." Madison, Wisc.: unpublished manuscript.

LUNBERG, FERDINAND
1969   *The Rich and the Super-Rich.* New York: Bantam.

LUTHE, HEINZ OTT
1968   "Record music and the music industry." *International Social Science Journal* 20:656–65.

LYND, ROBERT S.
1939   *Knowledge for What?* Princeton, N.J.: Princeton University Press.

———, and HELEN LYND
1929   *Middletown.* New York: Harcourt Brace Jovanovich.

———, and HELEN LYND
1937   *Middletown in Transition.* New York: Harcourt Brace Jovanovich.

MACAULAY, STEWART
1966   *Law and the Balance of Power: The Automobile Manufacturers and Their Dealers.* New York: Russell Sage Foundation.

McCARTHY, JOHN D. and WILLIAM L. YANCEY
1971   "Uncle Tom and Mister Charlie." *American Journal of Sociology* 76 (January):648–72.

MacGregor, James
  1969 "Boss men: Migrant workers find their lives controlled by farm crew leaders." *Wall Street Journal* (September 15):1, 25.

McLuhan, Marshall
  1962 *The Gutenberg Galaxy.* Toronto: University of Toronto Press.

  ———

  1964 *Understanding Media: The Extensions of Man.* New York: McGraw-Hill.

McPhee, William N.
  1966 "When culture becomes a business," in Joseph Berger, Morris Zelditch, Jr., and Bo Anderson (eds.), *Social Theories in Progress.* Boston: Houghton Mifflin.

Malabre, Alfred L., Jr.
  1968 "Inflation paradox: Analysts say prices rise fastest in fields lacking strong unions." *Wall Street Journal* (October 22):1, 12.

Mann, Floyd C. and L. R. Hoffman
  1960 *Automation and the Worker: A Study of Social Change in Power Plants.* New York: Holt, Rinehart & Winston.

Manne, Henry G.
  1965 "Mergers and the market for corporate control." *Journal of Political Economy* 73 (April):110–20.

Mannheim, Karl
  1941 *Man and Society in an Age of Reconstruction.* New York: Harcourt Brace Jovanovich.

Mantoux, Paul
  1961 *The Industrial Revolution in the Eighteenth Century: An Outline of the Beginnings of the Modern Factory System in England.* New York: Macmillan.

Manuel, Frank E.
  1956 *The New World of Henri Saint-Simon.* Cambridge, Mass.: Harvard University Press.

Marcson, Simon (ed.)
  1970 *Automation, Alienation, and Anomie.* New York: Harper & Row.

Marcuse, Herbert
  1967 *One-Dimensional Man: Studies in the Ideology of Advanced Industrial Society.* Boston: Beacon Press.

Marshall, Alfred
  1925 *Principles of Economics.* London: Macmillan.

  ———

  1948 *Principles of Economics.* New York: Holt, Rinehart & Winston.

MARX, KARL and FRIEDRICH ENGELS
   1848   *The Communist Manifesto.* Samuel H. Beer (ed.). New
          York: Appleton-Century-Crofts, 1955.
MATTHEISSEN, PETER
   1969   *Sal Si Puedes.* New York: Dell.
MAXWELL, NEIL
   1971   "Campaign to unionize textile plant splits sleepy southern town."
          Wall Street Journal (April 13):1, 10.
MAY, EDGAR
   1964   *The Wasted Americans.* New York: New American Library.
MAYER, KURT B. and SIDNEY GOLDSTEIN
   1964   "Manual workers as small businessmen" in Arthur. B. Shostak
          and William Gomberg (eds.), *Blue-Collar World.* Englewood
          Cliffs, N.J.: Prentice-Hall.
MEAD, DAVID
   1969   "Democratic centralism and decentralism as it relates to worker
          alienation in Russian agriculture," Nashville, Tenn.: unpub-
          lished manuscript.
MECHANIC, DAVID
   1962   "Sources of power of lower participants in complex organiza-
          tions." *Administrative Science Quarterly* 7 (December): 349–
          64.
MEIER, RICHARD L.
   1966   *Science and Economic Development.* Cambridge, Mass.:
          M.I.T. Press.
MEISLIN, BERNARD J. and MORRIS L. COHEN
   1964   "Backgrounds of the biblical law against usury." *Comparative
          Studies in Society and History* 6 (April):250–67.
MEISSNER, MARTIN
   1969   *Technology and the Worker: Technical Demands and Social
          Process in Industry.* Scranton, Pa.: Chandler.
MENDELSOHN, HAROLD and IRVING CRESPI
   1970   *Polls, Television, and the New Politics.* Scranton, Pa.: Chand-
          ler.
MERTON, ROBERT K.
   1968   *Social Theory and Social Structure.* New York: Free Press.
   ————, and ROBERT A. NISBET
   1971   *Contemporary Social Problems.* New York: Harcourt Brace
          Jovanovich.
MEYER, MARSHALL W.
   1968   "Automation and bureaucratic structure." *American Journal
          of Sociology* 74 (November):256–64.

MILL, JOHN STUART
1848 *Principles of Political Economy*. London: Longmans, Green.
MILLS, C. WRIGHT
1951 *White Collar: The American Middle Classes*. New York: Oxford University Press.

1959 *The Sociological Imagination*. New York: Oxford University Press.
MISHAN, E. J.
1970 *Technology and Growth*. New York: Praeger.
MONSON, R. JOSEPH, JR.
1963 *Modern American Capitalism: Ideologies and Issues*. Boston: Houghton Mifflin.
MONTAGNA, PAUL D.
1968 "Professionalization and bureaucratization in large professional organizations." *American Journal of Sociology* (September): 138–45.
MOORE, BARRINGTON, JR.
1966 *Social Origins of Dictatorship and Democracy: Lord and Peasant in the Making of the Modern World*. Boston: Beacon Press.
MOORE, WILBERT E.
1947 "Current issues in industrial sociology." *American Sociological Review* 12 (December):651–57.

1951 *Labor and Industrialization*. Ithaca, N.Y.: Cornell University Press.

1963 *Social Change*. Englewood Cliffs, N.J.: Prentice-Hall.

1965 *The Impact of Industry*. Englewood Cliffs, N.J.: Prentice-Hall.
MORSE, NANCY C. and EVERETT REIMER
1956 "The experimental change of a major organizational variable." *Journal of Applied Social Psychology* 28 (September):120–29.
MOSKIN, J. ROBERT
1969 "The new contraceptive society." *Look* (February 4):50–53.
MOYNIHAN, DANIEL P.
1968 "The crisis in welfare." *Public Interest* 10 (Winter):3–29.
MUELLER, EVA
1969 *Technological Advance in an Expanding Economy: Its Impact*

on a Cross-Section of the Labor Force. Ann Arbor: University of Michigan Press.

MYERS, CHARLES A. (ed.)
1967   *The Impact of Computers on Management*. Cambridge, Mass.: M.I.T. Press.

MYRDAL, GUNNAR
1966   *Beyond the Welfare State*. New Haven, Conn.: Yale University Press.

NADER, RALPH
1967   *Unsafe at any speed*. New York: Grossman.

NASH, MANNING
1966   *Primitive and Peasant Economic Systems*. Scranton, Pa.: Chandler.

Nashville Tennessean
1967   "Arrests cited: 'Shiners' linked to phony bills" (October 13): 11.

NEAL, ARTHUR G. and SOLOMON RETTIG
1963   "Dimensions of alienation among manual and nonmanual workers." *American Sociological Review* 28 (August):599–608.

NEFF, WALTER S.
1968   *Work and Human Behavior*. New York: Atherton.

NELSON, CLIFFORD C.
1969   *Black Economic Development*. New York: Columbia University Press.

New Republic
1966   "Coal fever." 15 (April 9):7.

NOBILE, PHILIP (ed.)
1971   *The Con III Controversy: The Critics Look at the Greening of America*. New York: Pocket Books.

NORTHROP, F.S.C.
1949   *The Meeting of East and West*. New York: Macmillan.

Occupational Outlook Handbook
1969   Washington, D.C.: United States Department of Labor, Bureau of Labor Statistics, Bulletin 1550.

O'CONNOR, HARVEY
1968   *World Crisis in Oil*. New York: Modern Reader.

O'DONNELL, JOHN A. and JOHN C. BALL (eds.)
1966   *Narcotic Addiction*. New York: Harper & Row.

OGBURN, WILLIAM FIELDING
1933   *Social Change*. New York: Viking Press.

OPSHAL, ROBERT L. and MARVIN D. DUNNETTE
  1966 "The role of financial compensation in industrial motivation."
        Psychological Bulletin 66 (February):94–118.
ORDEN, SUSAN R. and NORMAN M. BRADBURN
  1969 "Working wives and marriage happiness." *American Journal
        of Sociology* 74 (January):392–407.
PACEY, MARGARET D.
  1968 "Everything but the moo: What beef packers are using to
        fatten their profit margins." *Barron's Weekly* (July 22):3–22.
PARSONS, TALCOTT and NEIL J. SMELSER
  1956 *Economy and Society.* New York: Free Press.
PEARLSTINE, NORMAN
  1971 "GM offering temporary financing to AMC." *Wall Street
        Journal* (February 3):4.
PECK, MERTON J. and FREDERIC M. SCHERER
  1962 *The Weapons Acquisition Process: An Economic Analysis.*
        Cambridge, Mass.: Research Publication.
PECK, SIDNEY M.
  1963 *The Rank-and-File Leader.* New Haven, Conn.: New Haven
        College and University Press.
PELLING, HENRY
  1960 *American Labor.* Chicago: University of Chicago Press.
PENN, STANLEY
  1969 "A new breed of movie attracts the young, shakes up Holly-
        wood." *Wall Street Journal* (Nov. 14):1, 14.
PERLIN, LEONARD I.
  1962 "Alienation from work: A study of nursing personnel." *Ameri-
        can Sociological Review* 27 (June):314–26.
PERLMAN, MARK
  1958 *Labor Union Theories in America.* Evanston, Ill.: Row, Peter-
        son.
PERROW, CHARLES
  1967 "A framework for the comparative analysis of organizations."
        American Sociological Review 32 (April):194–208.

  1970 "Departmental power and perspectives in industrial firms," in
        Mayer N. Zald (ed.), *Power in Organizations.* Nashville,
        Tenn.: Vanderbilt University Press.
PERRUCCI, ROBERT and JOEL E. GERSTL
  1969 *Profession Without Community: Engineers in American So-
        ciety.* New York: Random House.

PETERSON, CLAIRE L.
    1970   "UFWOC: A new kind of union." Nashville, Tenn.: un-
    published manuscript.

PETERSON, HAROLD H.
    1970   *With the Indian Army in the Great War: 1916–1919.* Palo
    Alto, Calif.: privately published.

PETERSON, RICHARD A.
    1962a   "Review of human relations in management," by William G.
    Scott, *American Sociological Review* 27 (August):710–11.

———
    1962b   "The intellectual career of C. Wright Mills." *Wisconsin Sociol-
    ogist* 1 (Fall):17–29.

———
    1966   "Technological change, labor law, and managerial ideology:
    Co-determinants of the evolving rule of law in industry."
    Miami, Fla.: paper delivered to the American Sociological
    Association meetings.

———
    1970a   "Technology: Master, servant, or model for human dignity,"
    in Ruben Gotesky and Ervin Laszlo (eds.), *Human Dignity.*
    New York: Gordon & Breach.

———
    1970b   "Some consequences of differentiation," in Mayer N. Zald
    (ed.), *Power in Organizations.* Nashville, Tenn.: Vanderbilt
    University Press.

———, and DAVID G. BERGER
    1971   "Entrepreneurship in organizations: Evidence from the pop-
    ular music industry." *Administrative Science Quarterly* 16
    (March):97–107.

———, and DAVID G. BERGER
    1972   "Three eras in the manufacture of popular music lyrics," in
    R. Serge Denisoff and Richard A. Peterson (eds.), *The Sounds
    of Social Change.* Chicago: Rand McNally.

———, and LARRY DEBORD
    1966   *Educational Supportiveness of the Home and Academic Per-
    formance of Disadvantaged Boys,* IMRID Mono. III. Nash-
    ville, Tenn.: Peabody College Press.

———, and N. J. DEMERATH, III
    1965   "Introduction" to Liston Pope, *Millhands and Preachers.* New
    Haven, Conn.: Yale University Press.

————, and MICHAEL J. RATH
　1964　"Structural determinants of piecework rates." *Industrial Relations* 4 (October) :92–103.

PIRENNE, HENRI
　1937　*Economic and Social History of Medieval Europe.* New York: Harcourt Brace Jovanovich.

————
　1956　*Medieval Cities.* Garden City, N.Y.: Doubleday.

POPE, LISTON
　1965　*Millhands and Preachers.* New Haven, Conn.: Yale University Press.

PRESTHUS, ROBERT
　1962　*The Organizational Society.* New York: Knopf.

PROXMIRE, WILLIAM
　1966　"Wisconsin's economic future better because of new lease on life for American Motors." *Report from Washington* (October) :2.

PUGH, DEREK
　1966　"Role activation conflict: A study of industrial inspection." *American Sociological Review* 31 (December) :835–42.

PURSELL, CARROLL W., JR. (ed.)
　1969　*Readings in Technology and American Life.* New York: Oxford University Press.

RAAB, MARK
　1969　"Working class populism and the 1968 Wallace vote." Nashville, Tenn.: Vanderbilt University, Master's thesis.

RAMIRE, PAUL
　1969　"Slim pickings: Migrant farm hands strain for $1 an hour harvesting cucumbers." *Wall Street Journal* (September 19) :1, 10.

RANDALL, CLARENCE B.
　1961　*The Folklore of Management.* Boston: Little, Brown.

RAPOPORT, ROGER
　1967　"Life on the line: A week spent building cars gives an insight into industry's problems." *Wall Street Journal* (July 24) :1, 18.

RASKIN, A. H.
　1964　"Automation: Its impact on workers." *Saturday Review* (November) :14–16, 68.

REES, ALBERT
　1962　*The Economics of Trade Unions.* Chicago: University of Chicago Press.

REICH, CHARLES A.
   1970   *The Greening of America.* New York: Random House.

REYNOLDS, LARRY T. and JANICE M. REYNOLDS
   1970   *The Sociology of Sociology.* New York: McKay.

RICE, CHARLES D.
   1967   "Nineteenth century railroad technology, management, and government control." Nashville, Tenn.: unpublished manuscript.

RISCHIN, MOSES (ed.)
   1965   *The American Gospel of Success.* Chicago: Quadrangle.

RITTI, R. RICHARD
   1971   *The Engineer in the Industrial Corporation.* New York: Columbia University Press.

ROSS, ARTHUR and HERBERT HILL (eds.)
   1967   *Employment, Race, and Poverty.* New York: Harcourt Brace Jovanovich.

ROSSI, ALICE S.
   1968   "Transition to parenthood." *Journal of Marriage and Family* 30 (September) :26–39.

ROSTOW, W. W.
   1962   *The Stages of Economic Growth: A Non-Communist Manifesto.* New York: Cambridge University Press.

ROSZAK, BETTY and THEODORE ROSZAK (eds.)
   1969   *Masculine/Feminine: Readings in Sexual Mythodology and Liberation of Women.* New York: Harper & Row.

ROTTENBERG, DAN
   1969   "Eat-Out shake-out: fast-food places face fight for survival as franchised stands crowd roadsides." *Wall Street Journal* (September 10) :36.

ROY, DONALD F.
   1952   "Quota restriction and goldbricking in a machine shop." *American Journal of Sociology* 57 (March) :427–42.

   ———
   1953   "Work satisfaction and social reward in quota achievement: An analysis of piecework incentive." *American Sociological Review* 18:507.

RUSHING, WILLIAM A.
   1968a "Alcoholism and suicide rates by status set and occupation." *Quarterly Journal of Studies on Alcohol* 29 (June) :399–412.

   ———
   1968b "Objective and subjective aspects of deprivation in a rural poverty class." *Rural Sociology* 33 (September) :269–84.

1971 "Class, culture and 'Social structure and anomie!'" *American Journal of Sociology* 76 (March) :857–72.

RYSCAVAGE, PAUL M.
1967 "Changes in occupational employment over the past decade." *Monthly Labor Review* (August) :27–30.

SCHILLER, HERBERT I.
1969 *Mass Communications and the American Empire.* New York: Augustus Kelley.

SCHLIEWEN, ROLF
1970 "Cartel control of the Wankel patents," Nashville, Tenn.: unpublished manuscript.

SCHNEIDER, EUGENE V.
1969 *Industrial Sociology.* New York: McGraw-Hill.

SCHNEIDER, LOUIS
1950 "An industrial sociology—for what ends?" *Antioch Review* 10:117–29.

SCHON, DONALD A.
1967 *Technology and Change.* New York: Delacorte.

SCHONFELD, ANDREW
1965 *Modern Capitalism.* London: Oxford University Press.

SCHORR, BURT
1969 "Ailing entrepreneurs: Some U.S.-assisted black businesses lag after initial financing." *Wall Street Journal* (September 23): 1, 12.

1971a "Saving to U.S. from crop-subsidy limits, once put at $30 million, now seen far lower." *Wall Street Journal* (March 9): 28.

1971b "Black construction contractors find selves cut out of lucrative long-term contracts." *Wall Street Journal* (May 7) :22.

SCHUMPETER, JOSEPH A.
1934 *Theory of Economic Development.* Cambridge, Mass.: Harvard University Press.

1952 *Capitalism, Socialism and Democracy.* New York: Harper & Row.

SCOTT, WILLIAM G.
1965 *The Management of Conflict.* Homewood, Ill.: Irwin-Dorsey Press.

SEEMAN, MELVIN
1959 "On the meaning of alienation." *American Sociological Review* 24 (December) :783–91.

———
1967 "On the personal consequences of alienation in work." *American Sociological Review* 32 (April) :273–85.

SELIGMAN, BEN B.
1968 *Permanent Poverty.* Chicago: Quadrangle.

SELZNICK, PHILIP
1952 *The Organizational Weapon.* New York: McGraw-Hill.

———
1969 *Law, Society, and Industrial Justice.* New York: Russell Sage Foundation.

SETHI, S. PRAKASH
1970 *Business Corporations and the Black Man.* Scranton, Pa.: Chandler.

SHEMEL, SIDNEY and M. WILLIAM KRASIIOVSKY
1965 *This Business of Music.* New York: Billboard Press.

SHOSTAK, ARTHUR B.
1969 *Blue-Collar Life.* New York: Random House.

———, and WILLIAM GOMBERG (eds.)
1964 *Blue-Collar World.* Englewood Cliffs, N.J.: Prentice-Hall.

SIEGMAN, JACK and BERNARD KARSH
1962 "Some organizational correlates of white collar automation." *Sociological Inquiry* 32 (Winter) :108–16.

SILBERMAN, CHARLES E.
1966 *The Myths of Automation.* New York: Harper & Row.

SILVER, ALLAN
1966 "Military repression and political reform: British elite perspectives in 1828–1832," Evian, France, paper presented to the Sixth World Congress of Sociology.

SIMMONS, OZZIE G.
1965 *Work and Mental Illness.* New York: John Wiley.

SIMON, HERBERT A.
1965 *The Shape of Automation for Men and Management.* New York: Harper & Row.

SKOLNICK, ARLENE S. and JEROME H. SKOLNICK
1971 *Family in Transition.* Boston: Little, Brown.

SMELSER, NEIL J.
1959 *Social Change in the Industrial Revolution.* Chicago: University of Chicago Press.

1963 *Sociology of Economic Life.* Englewood Cliffs, N.J.: Prentice-Hall.

————, and JAMES A. DAVIS
1969 *Sociology.* Englewood Cliffs, N.J.: Prentice-Hall.

SMITH, ADAM
1776 *The Wealth of Nations.* New York: Modern Library, 1937.

SODERLIND, STERLING E.
1970 "Appraisal of current trends in business and finance." *Wall Street Journal* (January 12):1.

SORENSEN, ROBERT C.
1951 "The concept of conflict in industrial sociology." *Social Forces* 29 (March):263–67.

SPICER, EDWARD H. (ed.)
1952 *Human Problems in Technological Change: A Casebook.* New York: John Wiley.

Der Spiegel
1969 "Automobile konzentration: Zeit der giganten." (March 17): 70–77.

STABLER, CHARLES N.
1968 "Even accountants find some financial reports of combines baffling." *Wall Street Journal* (August 5):1, 12.

————
1969 "Concerns buying stock in other corporations face new legal peril." *Wall Street Journal* (February 24):1, 8.

STAVENHAGEN, RODOLFO
1967 "Seven erroneous theses about Latin America." *New University Thought* 4 (Winter):25–37.

STEARNS, PETER N.
1967 *European Society in Upheaval.* New York: Macmillan.

STEIN, MAURICE and ARTHUR VIDICH (eds.)
1963 *Sociology on Trial.* Englewood Cliffs, N.J.: Prentice-Hall.

STERN, JAMES L.
1967 "Unions and automation." *The Progressive* 31 (February): 24–26.

STEVENSON, ADLAI E.
1955 "My faith in democratic capitalism." *Fortune* (October): 6–7.

STINCHCOMBE, ARTHUR L.
1959 "Bureaucratic and craft administration of production: A comparative study." *Administrative Science Quarterly* 4 (September):168–87.

STONE, ROBERT C.
    1952   "Conflicting approaches to the study of worker-manager rela-
    tions." *Social Forces* 31 (December):117–24.
STOUT, THOMAS M.
    1962   "Process control: Past, present, and future." *Annals of the
    American Academy of Political and Social Science* 340
    (March):29–37.
STOVER, JOHN F.
    1961   *American Railroads.* Chicago: University of Chicago Press.
STRAUSS, GEORGE
    1968   "Human relations—1968 style." *Industrial Relations* 7 (May):
    262–75.
STURDIVANT, FREDERICH D.
    1969   "The limits of black capitalism." *Harvard Business Review*
    47 (January):118–28.
SULTAN, PAUL and PAUL PRASOW
    1964   "The skill impact of automation," reprinted from "Exploring
    the dimensions of the manpower revolution, vol. 1 of *Selected
    Readings in Employment and Manpower,* compiled for the
    Subcommittee on Employment and Manpower of the Com-
    mittee on Labor and Public Welfare, U.S. Senate.
SULZO, CHANDLER
    1968   "Graphic advance: Makers of printing equipment are updat-
    ing an age-old process." *Barron's National Business and Finan-
    cial Weekly* (July 20):4–6, 8.
SUTTON, CLAYTON
    1968   "Ghetto entrepreneurs: Negro businesses gain with sweat and
    loans." *Wall Street Journal* (October 7):1.
SUTTON, FRANCIS X., SEYMOUR E. HARRIS, CARL KAYSEN, and JAMES
TOBIN
    1956   *The American Business Creed.* Cambridge, Mass.: Harvard
    University Press.
TANZER, MICHAEL
    1969   *The Political Economy of International Oil and the Under-
    developed Countries.* Boston: Beacon Press.
TAVISS, IRENE
    1969   "Changes in the form of alienation: The 1900s vs. the 1950s."
    American Sociological Review 34 (February):46–57.
TAWNEY, R. H.
    1937   *Religion and the Rise of Capitalism.* New York: New Ameri-
    can Library.

TAYLOR, FREDERICK W.
1911   The Principles of Scientific Management. New York: Harper
       & Row.

THAYER, GEORGE
1969   The War Business: The International Trade in Armaments.
       New York: Simon & Schuster.

THERNSTROM, STEPHAN
1965   " 'Yankee City' revisited: The perils of historical naiveté."
       American Sociological Review 30 (April):234–42.

THOMPSON, E. P.
1963   The Making of the English Working Class. New York: Ran-
       dom House.

THOMPSON, JAMES D.
1967   Organizations in Action: Social Science Bases of Administra-
       tive Theory. New York: McGraw-Hill.

———, and ARTHUR TUDEN
1959   "Strategies, structures and processes of organizational deci-
       sion," in James D. Thompson, Peter B. Hammond, Robert W.
       Hawkes, Buford H. Junker, and Arthur Tuden (eds.), Com-
       parative Studies in Administration. Pittsburgh: University of
       Pittsburgh Press.

THRUPP, SYLVIA L.
1948   The Merchant Class of Medieval London. Ann Arbor: Uni-
       versity of Michigan Press.

Time
1969   "The little strike that grew to La Causa." (July 4): 16–21.

———
1969   "The conglomerate of crime." (August 22):17–27.

TUDOR, WILLIAM D.
1971   "Occupational bases of powerlessness," Nashville, Tenn.:
       Vanderbilt University, Ph.D. dissertation.

TYLER, GUS
1962   Organized Crime in America: A Book of Readings. Ann
       Arbor: University of Michigan Press.

UDRY, J. RICHARD
1971   The Social Context of Marriage. Philadelphia: Lippincott.

UDY, STANLEY H., JR.
1970   Work in Traditional and Modern Society. Englewood Cliffs,
       N.J.: Prentice-Hall.

UPHOFF, WALTER H.
1966   Kohler on Strike. Boston: Beacon Press.

VAN DE VALL, MARK
   1970   *Labor Organizations*. Cambridge, Mass.: Cambridge University Press.

VOLLMER, HOWARD M.
   1960   *Employee Rights and the Employment Relationship*. Berkeley: University of California Press.

———, and DONALD L. MILLS
   1962   "Nuclear technology and the professionalization of labor." *American Journal of Sociology* 67 (May):690–96.

VROOM, VICTOR H.
   1964   *Work and Motivation*. New York: John Wiley.

WALKER, CHARLES R. and ROBERT H. GUEST
   1952   "The man on the assembly line." *Harvard Business Review* 38 (May-June):71–83.

WARD, LESTER F.
   1907   *Pure Sociology*. New York: Macmillan.

WARNER, W. LLOYD and J. O. LOW
   1947   *The Social System of the Modern Factory: The Strike: A Sociological Analysis*. New Haven, Conn.: Yale University Press.

Washington Newsletter
   1968   "Who is helping whom?" Washington Newsletter of the Friends Committee on National Legislation 296 (August):8.

WATERMULDER, PAUL
   1969   "Developing black entrepreneurs," Nashville, Tenn.: unpublished manuscript.

WEBER, EUGENE (ed.)
   1965   *The Western Tradition*. Boston: Heath.

WEBER, MAX
   1947   *The Theory of Social and Economic Organization*. New York: Free Press.

———
   1958   *The Protestant Ethic and the Spirit of Capitalism*. New York: Scribner's.

———
   1961   *General Economic History*. New York: Collier.

WEIL, GORDON L.
   1968   "Many firms adopt new corporate symbols in bid to improve recognition, lift sales." *Wall Street Journal* (August 1):18.

WEINSTEIN, JAMES
   1968   *The Corporate Ideal in the Liberal State: 1900–1918*. Boston: Beacon Press.

WEIR, STANLEY
  1967   "USA—the labor revolt," *International Socialist Journal* 4
         (June) : 281–96.
WENNER, JANN
  1969   "The rolling stone interview: Phil Spector." *Rolling Stone*
         45 (November 1) : 22–29.
WESTLEY, WILLIAM A.
  1953   "Violence and the police," *American Journal of Sociology* 59
         (July) : 34–41.
WHISLER, THOMAS L.
  1970   *Information Technology and Organizational Change.* Bel-
         mont, Calif.: Wadsworth.
WHITE, LYNN, JR.
  1962   *Medieval Technology and Social Change.* Oxford, England:
         Oxford University Press.
WIEBE, ROBERT H.
  1968   *Businessmen and Reform.* Chicago: Quardrangle.
WIENER, NORBERT
  1966   *God and Golem Inc.* Cambridge, Mass.: M.I.T. Press.
WILENSKY, HAROLD
  1957   "Human relations in the workplace: An appraisal of some
         recent research," in Conrad Arensberg (ed.), *Research in
         Industrial Human Relations.* New York: Harper & Row.

  ———   1961   "The uneven distribution of leisure: The impact of economic
               growth on 'free time'." *Social Problems* 9 (Summer) : 32–56.

  ———   1963   "The moonlighter: A product of relative deprivation," *Indus-
               trial Relations* 3 (October) : 105–24.

  ———   1964a   "The professionalization of everyone?" *American Journal of
                Sociology* 70 (September) : 137–58.

  ———   1964b   "Varieties of work experience," in Henry Barow (ed.), *Man
                in a World at Work.* New York: Houghton Mifflin.

  ———   1967   *Organizational Intelligence: Knowledge and Policy in Gov-
               ernment and Industry.* New York: Basic Books.
WILLHELM, SIDNEY M. and ELWIN M. POWELL
  1964   "Who needs the negro?" *Trans-Action* I (September) : 3–6.
WINICK, CHARLES
  1968   *The New People.* New York: Pegasus.

WINTER, RALPH E.
  1970   "Factories begin to install versatile devices." *Wall Street Journal* (December 15):28.

WOLFBEIN, SEYMOUR L.
  1962   "Automation and skill." *Annals of the American Academy of Political and Social Science* 340 (March):53–59.

WYLLIE, IRVIN G.
  1966   *The Self-Made Man in America.* New York: Free Press.

ZAGRI, SIDNEY
  1966   *Free Press, Free Trial.* Chicago: Charles Hallberg.

ZALD, MAYER N.
  1971   *Occupations and Organizations in American Society.* Chicago: Markham.

ZEITLIN, IRVING M.
  1968   *Ideology and the Development of Sociological Theory.* Englewood Cliffs, N.J.: Prentice-Hall.

ZEITLIN, MAURICE
  1966   "Alienation and revolution." *Social Forces* 45 (December): 224–36.

Wall Street Journal
  December 1, 1967:1
    "Texas Instruments to transfer 25,000 onto salaried rolls."
  December 14, 1967:1, 13
    "Rural colossus: Farm bureau criticized anew for branching out into diversified fields."
  December 15, 1967:3
    "What's rotten in cotton?"
  December 26, 1967:1, 9
    "Grads in the shop: Complex technology spurs industry to turn to colleges for foremen."
  January 5, 1968:1
    "Crime and labor: Mobsters grab power in 16 teamster locals in the New York area."
  February 10, 1968:1
    "The outlook: Appraisal of current trends in business and finance."
  February 13, 1968:3
    "Ford acts to diversify in transport field: Railroad, highway ventures are studied."

February 29, 1968:5
"Auto makers acknowledge they can meet federal antismog standards for '70 models."

March 6, 1968:4
"Companies study substitutes for bottles as walkout by glass blowers drags on."

March 8, 1968:22
"Cartel in Pennsylvania: Army purchases of coal for German posts from price-fixing firms spark U.S. suit."

May 7, 1968:8
"Blue-collar unions push to organize public employees, including white-collars."

June 25, 1968:1, 9
"How violent are we? Social scientists find less strife in U.S. now than in past decades."

June 25, 1968:1
"Union politicos fear a drift to the right among the rank-and-file."

July 11, 1968:22
"Riot fear impact: Ghetto firms are hit by canceled insurance, higher rates: some forced out of business."

July 15, 1968:1, 19
"Laborers are enrolling diverse groups to fill gap left by automation."

July 25, 1968:1
"The conglomerates: Antitrusters, inventors eye combines warily, but firms still grow."

July 29, 1968:1
"You're the boss: a franchise operator finds rewards of life outweigh long hours."

August 5, 1968:3
"Corporate sodbusters: They are bringing financial and technological change to U.S. farming."

August 9, 1968:3
"U.S. steel plans to enter aluminum field by acquiring Alside for $39 million cash."

October 11, 1968:3
"Transamerica, Metromedia plan to consolidate, value of stock-swap accord put at about $300 million; FCC must back merger, Metromedia sells film unit."

October 15, 1968:5
"NLRB's ruling that Stevens used unfair labor practices is let stand by justices."

October 18, 1968:1, 17

"Blue-collar blues, a factory town survey confirms workingmen are bitter as vote nears, prices, taxes, poverty war, riots anger many; some defect from Democrats, discontent despite prosperity."

October 28, 1968:1

"Fifteen firms named in charges involving 2 drugs, concerns are said to have plotted to monopolize sale of Quinine and Quninidine."

February 10, 1969:1

"Current trends in business and finance."

February 21, 1969:1, 6

"Unions plan assault on companies lured by Mexico's low pay."

November 3, 1970:4

"GM said to have rights to Wankel engine: Mulls European expansion, Japanese moves."

November 24, 1970:30

"How local strikes curb GM production and could hurt Ford and Chrysler output."

December 21, 1970:3

"Antitrust study of energy field developing because of Nixon's dislike of oil price rise."

March 17, 1971:6

"New accounting rule seen giving fillip to some 1st quarter earning reports."

April 19, 1971:4

"Hearing on charges Performance Systems overstated income set Thursday by SEC."

INDEX